AN
Imperfect
Caregiver's
JOURNEY

DIANNE G. ALLEN

Dedication

To all the angels in my life,

To my children Lynn, Tom and John, and their wonderful wives Jennifer, Michelle, and Rachel, all are loved beyond measure.

To Daniella, Eddie, Mike, Susan, and Ros, dearest friends, and family in our hearts, to the healers, doctors, nurses, therapists, Jan, Vi and colleagues, to the kind strangers and unseen friends,

I express my deepest gratitude for your guidance and support at each step of my journey.

And with immense respect and affection, here's to the caregivers, whether they have chosen this role or have been thrust into it.

Thank you for your selfless devotion and endless demonstrations of love.

He gives power to the faint; and increases the might of those that lack strength. Those that rely upon God will receive renewed strength, as if they had the wings of an eagle; they will run, and not be weary; and they will walk, and not be faint. They will be given the strength to do what they must do.
Isaiah 40:29, 31*

Blessed are the merciful, kind, and generous; for they will obtain mercy and the favor of the Lord.
Matthew 5:7

When angels visit us, we do not hear the rustle of wings, nor feel the feathery touch of the breast of a dove; but we know their presence by the love they create in our hearts.
- Mary Baker Eddy

* Biblical references throughout this book reflect the author's understanding of the cited texts.

Contents

Introduction

Life was perfect. And then without warning, everything changed.

I was on top of the world, deeply in love with and married to a brilliant, successful, healthy man who loved me too. I ended up losing that man and discovered an even deeper, more fulfilling love that forever changed my understanding of purpose, commitment and joy.

At the age of forty-eight and considered to be approaching the prime of his life, my husband suffered a massive stroke which destroyed the full right side of his brain and resulted in left-side paralysis as well as other critical health issues.

By anyone's account, prior to the stroke, he was viewed as extremely handsome, fit, and intelligent. Five years younger than my husband, I was also active and healthy and already had an established progressive career as a director at one of the country's highest-rated luxury hotels. The name of the company alone conjured up images of romance and supreme elegance on an international scale. More importantly, I was a completely treasured, protected, and indulged wife, when suddenly our lives changed forever.

Initially, I prayed for my husband's survival for the few hours more it would take to get home from Mexico to his bedside. Then I prayed he'd make it through the night, the next night, all the other nights and the many challenges he faced throughout the following twenty- plus years.

I didn't realize until much later that my husband and I were each on our own journey, which neither of us was prepared to undertake. But then, how could we have been prepared for this?

Throughout this book, I've included passages and stories that were, and remain, meaningful to me. I've also shared some caregiver tips or, as they're now often called, "hacks" that I learned along the way. I hope they too, are helpful to you or the caregiver in your life.

I learned that unexpectedly, the crushing weight of caregiver responsibilities can fall upon anyone. There is no distinction made between the young and the old, the fit and the frail, the new caregiver's gender, or the individual's state of readiness to assume these duties. The role of caregiver lands where it will, without discrimination.

Everyone's situation and level of resources are different and each of us unique in our approach to dealing with the new challenges before us. The only common thread is that at a very deep level, the caregiver is now responsible for the well-being and perhaps even survival, of someone else.

Some of my journey has been quite difficult to share, but I do so with the hope that my experiences may help others work through their own challenges and perhaps, find some help and encouragement. Since everyone's needs vary, there's no perfect formula to overcome each challenge.

You must, and you will, find your own path to hope, healing, a return to joy and sincere gratitude for what comes your way.

This is simply my story, an imperfect caregiver's journey.

CHAPTER 1

That Was Then

*To everything there is a reason, a season,
and a time for every purpose under heaven.*
Ecclesiastes 3:1

August 12, 1994

I was at the top of my game.

I was the exceptionally proud and happy wife of EJ Allen, a brilliant software engineer with the U.S. Space Program whose career prospects were equally bright. Our marriage of ten years was a happy one. Our life was quite comfortable, and based upon EJ's awards and meaningful progressive assignments, it was clear that our family's future was secure.

My three children—EJ's stepchildren—were on a solid path to becoming loving and accomplished adults. I was sure they would each make positive differences in the world. Spoiler alert: all have exceeded my hopes and dreams for them. Also, each has married an extraordinary, intelligent, and loving woman who has blessed us with ting grandchildren.

d a very satisfying career as an executive with international luxury hotel company. I was work and enjoyed telling my family and friends about my experiences. In retrospect, I probably bored them a little too much with the retelling of my fabulous life and adventures. Although, I'm not really sure; maybe it was a draw, because I also listened to their countless "beautiful family, exquisite life" stories.

After all, that's what friends do.

EJ's recent promotion was a three-year assignment at a location just outside of New Orleans. He was to assist the team to complete the work needed to fulfill a contract with the space agency. Afterwards, according to his employer's plan, we would return to central Florida, and EJ would assume another position at the Kennedy Space Center. Fortunately, within the same week of his appointment to the Louisiana project, I was offered a director's position with the only five-star property currently in New Orleans.

The timing couldn't have been better!

There are so many reasons why everyone loves New Orleans: the music, the art, the history, but most of all, the wonderful people. We quickly became immersed in our community and enjoyed many professional and social relationships. Our home was always filled with visiting family and friends. And while the first two years there flew by quickly, we also dreamt of returning home to Florida.

One particular day, I was at the luxurious Ritz Carlton Hotel in Cancun, Mexico, attending my company's annual executive retreat along with my colleagues. Our opening team-building event was a friendly, yet highly competitive, game of volleyball. This was followed by icy cold pitchers of beer and margaritas at the pool bar.

Despite the whirling of the giant palm frond ceiling fan overhead, my face flushed bright red. This prompted one of the guys to ask me if I was getting too much sun. I responded that I was fine, concealing the fact that in reality, I was flushed with pleasure from the intrusive thought that I would soon be back home and resting in my husband's strong arms.

The afternoon's business meetings were challenging, yet still productive. Afterward, I was more than a little self-satisfied that I had managed to carry my share of the responsibilities to develop strategic plans to further the hotel's success. I also held my own when my ideas were challenged and was able to ultimately engage the others to support every one of my proposals. Sadly, times were different then for women in the workplace, so this was no small feat to accomplish as the only woman on a team of highly successful alpha males.

After a long, intense day, the evening was capped by a celebratory night on the town, including good food, shared laughter, and a visit to a popular club, where we all joined the exuberant crowd to dance the Macarena.

We returned to the resort in the wee hours of the morning. After saying my quick goodnights to everyone, I headed straight for my suite. Without delay, I sank into the sumptuous bed and thought about my family back home, before drifting peacefully off to sleep.

Life was perfect. We had it all, a wonderful family, a beautiful home, good jobs.

Who wouldn't want to be us; who wouldn't want to be me?

The First Call

This day's team-building event was held at a luxury golf course affiliated with the Ritz. We arrived by VIP shuttle and were quickly escorted by the marshal to the first hole. After dropping us off, he headed back to the clubhouse, just as rapidly.

Hotel executives' lives are all about status and protocol so, of course, the managing director was the first to tee off. As a pure courtesy, I would be the second to start.

As I awaited my turn to begin play, the marshal suddenly reappeared. He was very solemn, as he pulled me aside to deliver the urgent message that I was to contact my home hotel immediately. I explained to my colleagues why I needed to step away and promised to rejoin them as soon as possible. At the time, we all assumed that my input was needed on a critical employee-related issue. My friends continued their game, while I was driven back to the clubhouse.

I returned the call to the hotel's manager on duty and was immediately put through. She gravely informed me there had been a medical emergency with EJ. Although she claimed not to know the details, she had been told it was unlikely he would make it through the next few hours, and if he did, in all probability, he wouldn't make it through the night.

At that moment, all around me ceased to exist.

Suddenly, I was in a steep and rapid fall into a seemingly unending black hole. I descended into a swirling vortex of blurred, scattered images, thoughts, and prayers. I heard only my loud, pounding heartbeat, saw nothing through the black fog that surrounded me and felt nothing other than my throbbing brain. I tried to ignore the rising bile in my throat. Weak at the knees, I collapsed on the nearby stairsteps, phone still in hand. I have no concept of how much time I spent on those stairs, for I remained there completely immobilized until one of my colleagues came to check on me.

Separately, the Ritz executives and my coworkers had also been notified of the emergency. Without my knowledge, they contacted the airline, made all travel arrangements for an immediate flight back to New Orleans and had a limousine waiting to take me directly to the hospital where EJ was being treated.

I was numb and disconnected from my surroundings as others shepherded me through every step of the journey. Initially, a very skeptical customs agent questioned why I was traveling without luggage.

"My husband is dying in Mandeville." Somehow through the fog of emotions, I managed to respond. I was immediately allowed to pass through and connect with the awaiting limo driver, provided by my home hotel.

Crossing the more than twenty-four-mile Lake Pontchartrain Causeway Bridge seemed to take hours. At the time, the Causeway was the world's longest bridge and was so huge that travelers lost sight of land during their drive to the other side of the lake. Prior to this journey,

I'd always felt quite at peace as I made the trip to and from New Orleans on a twice-daily basis. However, as I sat in the limo's backseat during this crossing, I felt totally lost in time and space as I stared at the water and prayed, I'd soon be home in Mandeville and once again at my husband's side.

There's been a big mistake. Everything will be all right. I just need to get to EJ, I tried to convince myself, as I listened to the rippling water lap up against the pylons of the bridge.

I had no way of knowing I hadn't hit the bottom yet and my upward journey to find some version of "normalcy" once again would last for decades.

CHAPTER 2

The Hospital, Early Days

Our Lord is ever present. He goes before me;
he is with me, he will not fail me, neither forsake
me: I have no reason to fear, nor to be discour-
aged. God is with me; this is all I need.
Deuteronomy 31:8

Just as a mother comforts her child,
so will I comfort you. I love you that much.
Isaiah 66:13

For in you O Lord, do I hope and I know
that you hear me without fail, O Lord my God.
Psalm 38:15

Drowning in a swirl of emotions, concerns, and questions, my first priority after arriving at the hospital was to comfort my children and get to my husband's bedside.

John, my youngest son, was standing before the window outside of EJ's room. I'll remember forever that first image of him. Although he was a tall, athletic teenager, he now looked so very young, small, frightened, and helpless. His older brother and sister had not yet arrived from out of state where they were attending college. During the preceding critical hours, John had been on his own and was now a drained shell of himself. He was devastated and had an all too true, haunted look.

It would be years before I would come to understand the true source and depth of his pain. As a mother, I still feel so much regret that I wasn't able to shield him from this experience.

As our eyes met, they said so much more than words could convey; he didn't try to hide his feelings, as he collapsed in my arms. We were both terrified.

"He's going to be okay, and we are going to be okay. I promise." I did what parents so often do for their children. I lied and tried to hide my own fears.

I then took a deep breath and mustered up all the courage I had before entering my husband's room, alone.

The last beams of twilight seeped through the spaces between the closed blinds, painting the room in a gloomy gray light. I could barely see EJ, ashen and unmoving, under the thin, white bed covers. Wires, tubes, and machines were attached to his seemingly lifeless form.

He was a pale shadow of the man I'd kissed goodbye just two days earlier. Without thought or hesitation, I jumped into the bed, climbed under the covers, laid my head upon his chest, and held his comatose body as tightly as I could. I prayed for his recovery with all my heart and soul.

I had no sense of time and didn't know how long I had been at EJ's side. I wasn't aware a doctor had entered the room at some point, until he cleared his throat to get my attention. He then scolded me and harshly ordered me to get out of my husband's bed.

Rightly or wrongly, I wasn't going to move, and they would need to call security to pry me away from EJ's bed.

"I'm not moving." My voice was steady, low, and cold. I didn't make eye contact with the doctor.

The doctor moved closer to me and, in an angrier voice than before, again told me to get out of my husband's bed. Once again, I ignored the order and held on even tighter.

An empathetic nurse eventually interceded and asked the doctor to leave me alone.

I'm not sure whether the doctor was influenced by the nurse or simply lost patience with the whole situation. It didn't really matter to me; I wasn't moving away from my husband's side.

The doctor eventually relented and left the room in a huff.

Oddly, I don't remember anything else about the doctor, yet I can still clearly envision the "no- nonsense" look the nurse gave him. I will be forever thankful for her kind interference and, as a result, the avoidance of additional unneeded drama and further emotional damage for our family.

I continued my prayers as I listened to my husband's faint heartbeats.

Eventually it became evident, even to me, that it was impractical for me to remain in the bed next to my husband's still, cool, unresponsive body. The medical staff needed to tend to him, and I left to provide a lot of critical information to the hospital administrators. Still feeling like I was trapped in a bad dream, I struggled to understand the staff's questions and provide coherent responses.

However, later that night, there was one statement I understood quite clearly.

"I'm very sorry, Mrs. Allen. You should prepare yourself; your husband may not make it through the night."

Trying to ignore the twisting railroad spike plunged through my heart, I prayed with all my being that the doctor was wrong.

During the longest night of our lives, I stayed by my husband's side holding his hand, which felt like frozen marble, praying for a miracle. I fervently prayed that my faith was enough.

Even though I knew better, I tried to make several deals with God, including, *Take me, not him. Bring him back to me and I promise I will . . .*

Seemingly against all odds, EJ made it through that night and the next and the next. He remained in a coma for some time. I don't recall how long, but I think it was about a week or maybe it was a few weeks. Much of that time still remains a grayish blur to me.

Throughout the following days, all I wanted was to have peace, be at EJ's side and have my children close to us. But none of us were to be granted this space.

There was much business to attend to, beginning with our extensive family. The calls to immediate family were the most difficult. We shared our shock, confusion, pain, and tears. However, none of us gave voice to our greatest fear; maybe he wouldn't make it.

This pattern was repeated over and over and over again, as I made each of these personal calls.

Whether it was because of the lack of sleep, poor nutrition, or stress, I soon realized that I wasn't myself. I had forgotten which calls I'd already made and those I'd spoken with before. In other cases, I remembered speaking with the person but forgot the content of our recent conversations.

Unfortunately, more than once I forgot about travel plans, we'd discussed. As a consequence, I was repeatedly surprised and unprepared when an out-of-state family member arrived at the hospital. They had to remind me that we'd agreed to the visit days before.

Out of sheer necessity, I eventually developed a cheat sheet of names, contact numbers and notes about our last conversations. I was still in such a fog that some days, the best I could do was check off the names of people I'd spoken with. That alone was a help.

I came to rely upon this simple log as a way to preserve at least one little corner of my sanity.

In the days that followed, a constant stream of medical professionals tried to explain my husband's condition to me, and they asked an exhausting number of questions.

Unavoidably, their attempts to help me understand EJ's conditions involved swamping me with information. I could only understand bits and pieces of what I was told including massive stroke, aneurysm, lost full right side of his brain, full left side paralyzed, lost forever, and highly improbable survival. But try as they might to help me understand the issues, I couldn't fully grasp what these things meant about his future and the impact on our family.

There was so much to understand, that I often became overwhelmed, couldn't absorb anymore, and would shut down completely. Yet, the person before me kept talking, sounding as if they were in an echo chamber, far away from me.

No wonder I felt lost and alone, trapped in a nightmare. I was.

EJ showed no visible signs of progress during the next few weeks. Quite the opposite, I was told several more times that he wasn't expected to make it through the night. I didn't believe them and yet the fear that they just might be right, lingered.

I realized, in truth, I was afraid to believe them; so, I *couldn't* believe them. I was afraid that somehow, if I gave up hope, all would end. So, I denied every assertion that my husband would soon die, put my faith in God and prayed with all my might.

I spent the long, endless nights in the chair next to EJ's bed. Sleep eluded me while an unending, repeating list of "What ifs" ran through my mind . . .

What if I hadn't gone on the trip? Would I have been able to help him more?

What if the EMTs had administered oxygen?

What if he'd been taken to a different hospital?

What if the doctor in charge of that shift had not put a "Do Not Contact" order on receiving phone messages?

Should I sue the EMTs? What should I do about that doctor in charge? Should I sue her, too?

Who should I call?

What's going to happen to us?

These and so many more questions plagued me.

Like a bad song stuck in my brain, these thoughts ran through my mind on an unending loop. I had no answers, only guilt, regret, anger, and tears.

I met countless times with administrative staff who needed a lot of information to ensure the hospital would get paid. They asked for documents, IDs, employer information, etc. Then came the questions about living wills, powers of attorney, end-of-life directives and other equally scary things.

While I did what I could, I wasn't prepared to answer many of these questions.

We'd never thought that far ahead.

Frequently, loving friends and family called for the latest updates. This meant I had to retell what little I knew, over and over again. I often felt inadequate in my ability to repeat the information I'd been given. I was personally struggling with denial, unfamiliar with even the most basic medical terms, while also attempting to remain positive. At the same time, I tried to comfort the caller and avoided the truth about my own state of mind and fears.

"Thank you, we're fine. I know; he loves you too. We're going to be okay, and we're just waiting for the news that he can come home soon. Thank you for keeping us in your prayers." With few variations, my script for these calls was always the same.

One person, however, didn't get the same response.

Once, when returning from a walk to the cafeteria for a cup of coffee, I found John on the phone next to EJ's bed. He looked very upset and was barely speaking to the person on the other end. Without explaining who he was talking with, he quickly handed me the phone and stepped back several feet.

"Hello, this is Dianne. Who is this please?"

The voice explained she was the lady who ran the local snowball stand, and although we didn't really know each other, she said she felt a connection to us, because her kids knew my son. She continued to explain she was calling to see if John was okay, after being the one to find his father in such a horrible way.

Without a pause, she excitedly probed for more information and was particularly interested in the gory details of the event.

"Is it true John was the one who found your husband naked on the bathroom floor? We heard he had been there for hours before he was found. Did he really pull the shower door off the hinges and make it crash on top of himself? It must have been horrible. Did the glass break? I heard there was so much blood all over the place. Lord! That must have been awful! Did it freak John out?" She hurriedly continued asking for more personal details that even family members hadn't broached. In fact, as I had gone straight from the airplane to the hospital, she apparently knew specifics about what happened in our home that I didn't even know yet.

It quickly became very clear to me that SnowBall Lady was motivated by her own ghoulish curiosity, not care and concern for my loved ones. I also realized that, in this small town, there were basically only two degrees of separation between all of us.

Everyone knew someone, who knew something and that "something" had great value on the gossip train. In the tradition of trade deals, you had to give some new tidbit to get something in return. By the level of details SnowBall Lady spewed, it was evident one of the EMTs had shared information about the incident with her. No one else had been inside our home and on the scene of EJ's collapse.

Unfortunately, at last I understood a saying of my grandmother's. "A dog never brings a bone, but it takes one home."

As SnowBall Lady continued to babble and press for more information, I remained quiet. I'm not sure whether my silence was because I was drained or in deep shock at the intrusiveness of this near stranger. However, it felt like an eternity before she either noticed I wasn't responding, or she simply ran out of steam.

Finally, I spoke, barely above a whisper.

"Leave us alone. DO NOT call my husband's room again and NEVER speak to my son again. Not only that, but if I hear that you've been talking about our family or making up big stories to make yourself look important in some sick way, I will personally take you out. And by the way, I know a lot about your little cash business. Got it?"

"Understood." SnowBall Lady's raspy whisper was barely audible as I hung up the phone.

As I turned to see my son, I was struck by the difference in his appearance from just moments before. His desperately stressed look had been replaced with one of love and appreciation. I'm not sure, but there may have also been a little admiration shining through his eyes. At least, that's how I remember it.

I'm not in the habit of bullying people, and of course, the comment about her cash business was an idle threat. I didn't know her as anything other than a nodding acquaintance, but as anyone in New Orleans could tell you about cash-only businesses, it was a safe bet she hadn't been entirely transparent in her business dealings. I really didn't care; I just wanted her to leave us alone.

I didn't know it at the time, but she would never trouble us again. Nor did anyone else from the neighborhood pursue any sad, personal details about our family. At least not to my face.

I had just experienced a necessary shift in my dealings with others that I didn't know I was capable of undertaking.

I learned from this experience to be more alert and discerning about others' motives. I became even more protective of my family and less tolerant of those who placed their own interests ahead of the well-being of my loved ones.

This wasn't the only thing I had to learn quickly. In addition to my familiar roles as a wife and mother, I now needed to have expertise in patient advocacy, benefits administration, as well as personal legal and financial matters. I also had to communicate with family, friends and employers and provide appropriate updates. Sometimes I wasn't sure what to share about the current situation and what to spare others from learning in reference to my husband's health issues and prognosis for recovery.

No matter how many kindnesses were shown to me, I often felt alone, confused and overwhelmed.

It was a daunting and terrifying time. I sobbed myself to sleep almost every night. I just wanted to wake up from the nightmare and feel safe in my husband's arms, once more.

Yet, no matter how much I tried to rally, nothing prepared me for the often-blunt comments I received from family, friends, and those I had to deal with in their professional capacity. I was told several times that their harsh words were "for my own good" and that my life with my husband was over; it was time for me to move on.

They were wrong, and this was proven again and again over the next twenty-plus years.

Our time together wasn't over; it just became different.

Our new journey was just beginning.

STEPPINGSTONES

∾ I don't get to choose what comes my way, but I can choose how to respond to each challenge.

∾ It's not rude to stand firm against aggressive, ill-intentioned people. It's not only my right, but also my duty to protect my loved ones from such as these.

∾ I trust that God will always give me the strength and guidance to do what I need to do; I am sustained by this faith, no matter how difficult it may be. Don't give up on God, who will never give up on me.

CHAPTER 3

First Things First

*I am with you always and you are with me
throughout eternity.*
Matthew 28: 20

*You pray in your distress and in your need;
would that you might pray also in the fullness
of your joy and in your days of abundance.*
- Khalil Gibran

Is prayer your steering wheel or your spare tire?
- Corrie ten Boom

*Prayer is not asking. Prayer is putting oneself in
the hands of God, at His disposition, and listening
to His voice in the depth of our hearts.*
- Mother Teresa

*Rejoice openly, share your joy with others,
pray without ceasing, in everything give thanks;
for this is the will of God.*
1 Thessalonians 5:16-18

Prior to my husband's stroke, I thought I had a good, comfortable, working relationship with God. I didn't bother

Him with the small stuff. My side of the equation primarily consisted of me remembering to say please and thank you at all the right times. It was all sunshine, light, and love between us. But then, my faith had never really been tested.

That first phone call forever changed my understanding and acknowledgement of the deeper need for God in my life.

Throughout my years as a caregiver, I experienced a profound rollercoaster of emotions including, among others, overwhelming sadness, joy, gratitude, doubt, deep anger at God and guilt. Periodically, I questioned my entire relationship with God or, rather, His to me.

Yet, I've also experienced a profoundly deep, glorious, and healing connection with God and an understanding that I am loved, at all times, under all circumstances. I'd never experienced such confusing extremes before but was told this is normal, especially during times of personal crisis.

Our family was most certainly in crisis.

Nothing made sense to me anymore, but that didn't matter. I didn't get to opt out of the situation. I had to keep pushing forward while I tried to figure things out.

My mind was overflowing with so many, seemingly perpetual questions no one could answer.

How could this happen to my husband? To our family?
What's going to happen?
Will he be okay? Will we be okay?
What do I need to do?
I know God loves us and will heal him, but if so, why do we have to go through this?
This isn't right. This isn't fair! Why us?

However, even in the midst of all this chaos, I was also frequently moved to tears with joy and gratitude for the little victories, experienced step by step. Amongst them, the first time my husband opened his eyes, weeks later the movement of a finger, an attempt to speak, a reach out to touch my face...

These seemingly small changes affected me deeply. With each one, I experienced renewed hope that all would soon be well; my husband would return to me, and everything was going to be all right again.

However, these physical advances were often fleeting, and their transitory nature impacted me greatly. At these times, I felt that sustaining hope for healing progress was like trying to catch a swiftly running brook between my fingers. Just when I thought I had caught it, hope slipped away again. Each setback left me crestfallen, and my spirits sunk to an even lower level than before.

I had not yet learned to never give up faith, regardless of what may appear to be the current circumstances.

Ricocheting between these thoughts and emotions, often at hyper speed, I was exhausted and seldom at peace. Ever so slowly, I began to understand that even the best recovery process may not be linear—or at least that was our experience.

Seemingly, EJ's recovery was a half-step forward, three back, one step forward, two back, and so on. This was the dance we would be engaged in for years. In retrospect, although often filled with disappointments and fear, what a blessing it was to have had that prolonged time together!

My own progress as a caregiver followed a similar pattern to my husband's experience; one step forward, three back, two forward, one back...I was engaged in this convoluted dance for years.

There was so much to learn, so much to do, so many decisions to make. Some things I did well, just by relying upon my intuition. Others were mistakes—some of which I could correct, others could not be undone.

Admittedly, I'm an imperfect human, so it follows that I've never been a perfect caregiver.

Is there such a person?

My husband got sick, but I was the same person as I was before the event. I didn't suddenly become all-wise, courageous and infallible. Despite some of my better qualities, I still made bad decisions, lost my patience, felt inadequate, and got angry that I'd been cheated out of a happy life. While putting up a strong front, I longed for someone to take care of ME and make my troubles disappear. And then, I'd feel guilty for thinking such selfish thoughts; after all, EJ had to deal with far bigger problems than mine.

No one could help me because I didn't share what was really going on with me. I thought it was so much more important to be brave and appear to have it all under control.

I was wrong.

The kindnesses of others helped to dull some of the pain but never fully changed the deep, empty pit where my heart used to be.

It was often very difficult, but no matter the ups and downs, ultimately, these experiences only deepened my understanding that I am truly a child of God, as are you. I pressed on through these trials and tried to remember even at the darkest of times, we don't get a vote; no matter our failings and questions, we are still loved.

Whatever your faith, traditions or understanding of your walk with God, now is the time to pray without ceasing and humbly accept all prayers. If your loved one is a different religion (as was our case), now is not the time for earthly conceived partisanships.

There is one God—the God of all. Welcome spiritual support, but also guard and defend your thoughts against messages that are not aligned with your own core values and beliefs.

It is never too late nor too complicated to commune with God in your own, personal way.

No matter how the immediate circumstances may present the situation, pray without ceasing.

When you've fallen to your knees from weakness and despair, pray.

Before you speak with others regarding the cared one's condition or treatment, pray.

When you're angry with God, pray.

When you're frustrated with yourself or others, pray.

When you're frightened, pray.

When you think you can't make it through another night, pray.

When there's been a demonstration of progress and healing, pray.

When you're lost, confused or doubtful, pray.

When you're lonely, pray.

When you're grateful, pray.

Every step of the way, pray, trust Him, praise Him.

So, what is prayer? It's our personal communion with God. It's the most intimate relationship we will ever have. No matter what you believe, it's just you and God having a conversation with nowhere to hide.

Others may include you and your loved ones in their prayers; some may even first ask for your permission. Regardless of any religious differences between you, express your simple gratitude for all offers. If not the words, embrace their heartfelt messages.

When the hospital chaplain comes by to pray over your loved one, welcome her.

When the priest who is there for another patient stops to speak with you, welcome him.

When friends tell you they are holding you all in prayer, thank them.

When a neighbor tells you they've included your family in their prayer chain, express your gratitude.

When you see a cardinal, fresh blooming flowers, or a loving light in someone else's eyes, or you hear a child's laughter, thank God for these gifts of love and beauty.

Express your gratitude openly and repeatedly. If you feel it, share it.

Your gratitude expressed will both bless others and bless yourself.

STEPPINGSTONES

- ∾ We are sustained by our faith.

- ∾ Pray without ceasing.

- ∾ Be grateful for God's love and all that entails, in advance of my need.

- ∾ Begin each day with Psalm 118:24. "This is the day the Lord has made; let us rejoice and be glad in it."

- ∾ End each night with the Lord's Prayer, understanding that the first word is *Our* and praying for all of us.

CHAPTER 4

Understanding Different Stages of Care

I will restore your health,
and I will heal your wounds.
Jeremiah 30:17

Stand still, consider the wondrous works
of God, and give thanks.
Job 37:14

O Lord my God, we cried unto you,
and you have healed us. Thank you, Father.
Psalm 30:2

I am the oldest of seven children. Ours was an active, busy, healthy and frequently expanding family. Thankfully, not one of us ever experienced a serious illness, broken bone or had any need to go to the hospital. Consequently, I grew up thinking of hospitals as simply big buildings where all mothers go to have babies.

Until my husband's critical medical event, I had only a surface-level understanding of the different types of care provided by a variety of facilities. Without knowing anyone who was a caregiver, no mentor was available to help me transition into my new role. However, through experience alone, I would soon learn much more about each facility and team's specific functions.

Throughout the years and while we lived in several different states, my husband experienced a variety of critical medical events. He was rushed to an emergency room, admitted, and readmitted to the hospital, went into ICU, and stayed in a semi-private room and skilled nursing facility, as needed. Based upon his current needs, he was also in and out of a variety of facilities specializing in therapy and received different levels of home care. Eventually, he resided in a long-term care facility on a permanent basis.

Obviously, the treating physician decides what level of care is needed, but as we would experience throughout his recovery from the initial stroke, your insurance coverage may also be a deciding factor in determining what resources and benefits are available for the patient. You may be asked for your preference in location but will not be able to negotiate the type of facility you prefer.

While titles or classifications may vary from state to state, here is a broad overview of the types of facilities and treatments available, based upon the individual's needs.

Hospital

- Emergency Room for urgent medical issues; it is not a "Quick Clinic" for routine issues.

    o Immediate assessment and care
    o Time-critical care

- ICU

    o Intensive Care Unit where patients need special medical care and are watched very closely.

- Room type may be assigned based upon your insurance coverage, your ability to pay or availability.

    o Private; lone patient

    o Semi-private; two to four patients

    o Ward: large room to accommodate multiple patients

- In-patient rehabilitation is offered by some hospitals.

Skilled Nursing Facility

It helps to think of a skilled nursing facility as providing care for the patient during a transition from the hospital to home care. The patient is medically stable but still needs a level of care that can't be provided at the next facility or at home.

- Ordered by a physician.
- Provides 24/7 nursing staff in an in-patient facility.
- Provides medical oversight and treatment for those who are not yet physically able to go home or transfer to another facility.
- May provide rehabilitation therapy according to the patient's needs.
- The length of stay may be time bound by both the physician and the insurance company, so it's criti-

cal to have conversations with the current facility about the anticipated next steps.

As much as you might want your loved one home, you may not be ready to take on the level of care required.

Also, you may feel that the best solution for both of you is to receive approval for an extended stay at the current facility. Express your concerns and preferences, however, you may not have a choice. The physician and the insurance company will dictate the timing of the transfer or release of the patient.

Rehabilitation Center

- Ordered by a physician.
- Provides a variety of therapies on premises; these may include physical, occupational and/or speech therapies.
- May or may not be outpatient only.

In-home Care

- Variety of services, dependent upon the patient's needs
- Some services may be covered by Medicare, Medicaid, and any additional patient coverage.
- Two basic categories

  o Health-related (ordered by a physician)

  - Therapists
  - Nursing services

- Assistance with medicine, in-line drips etc.

o Non-medical caregivers (see separate section on selecting and maintaining professional caregivers). A caregiver is responsible for the safety and well-being of the person in their charge. Duties may include:

- General oversight/companionship
- Housekeeping duties
- Light meal preparations
- Assistance with activities of daily living functions

Long-term Care

It may be very difficult to consider long-term care for your loved one. Still, there may come a time when you can no longer deny that others may be able to provide a better level of care than you can.

Whether it was wise or not, I prolonged the decision for as many years as I was able. Ultimately, the doctors determined that my husband's condition had declined to the point that there was no other option than admission to a long-term care facility.

Although our separation was quite painful, in time I realized that long-term care was the best option for both of us. He received the specialized care and medical oversight I could not provide at home. Slowly, I too experienced benefits I hadn't anticipated. My own health improved, and I was no longer in possible danger of injury while caring for my husband.

No matter the sadness I carried with me every day, I was comforted to know my husband was now in safer surroundings.

- There are a large variety of options for long-term care. (See separate section regarding the selection of a long-term care facility.)
- If the patient is experiencing dementia, Alzheimer's or a condition with similar impact, a facility with a memory care unit may be required. This will ensure the patient receives the appropriate attention and is secure within their environment.

Hospice/Comfort Care

May be needed at the end of life's journey.

- Services for the terminally ill and their families are provided.
- Provides physical (palliative) care.
- Supports family and patient spiritually and emotionally.

God bless the healers and caregivers!

I am humbled by those medical professionals and caregivers who elect these roles. They are not motivated by a personal connection, be it a family member or a friend, but by a pure desire to help others. I can think of no higher quality than to charitably choose a life of service to others, particularly at this critical time in another's life journey.

They are the true angels on earth.

STEPPINGSTONES

～ It's important for me to understand the stages and options for care.

～ Understanding the different functions of the various facilities and working with those teams helps me to better prepare for each step and maximize the outcomes for my loved one.

～ I may have input on the many important decisions concerning my husband's care, but not control. It's okay and safe to let the professionals guide me through this.

CHAPTER 5

In Care

Father, though I walk through the valley
of the shadow of death, I will fear no evil: for you
are always with me; you will lead me through this.
Your strength, love and your wisdom comfort me.
Psalm 23:4

I have come to understand that neither death,
nor life, nor principalities, nor powers,
nor the actions of others, nor things present,
nor things to come, nor height, nor depth,
nor any other creature, are able to separate us
from the love of God,
which is in Christ Jesus our Lord.
Romans 8:38-39

I am never alone because the Father is with me.
John 16:32

Usually, no one would be grateful that their loved one would require a long-term stay in the hospital.

But I was.

At this stage in our new upside-down world, each day under professional care meant the gift of another day of life for my husband. And I was learning how to navigate

my ever-changing role as both his support and advocate. Advocate, however, may not be a strong enough word for what was actually required of me at this point in my caregiver career.

"Activist" and all that implies would be a much better job description.

This wasn't a job I would ever seek, but it's the one I got. In fact, based upon my total lack of medical understanding and patience, I was uniquely *un*qualified to be a caregiver, but I did my best. Many times, that didn't feel good enough, but in the long run, it was.

During EJ's early days/weeks in the hospital, there was little for me to do but pray without ceasing, hold his hand and speak with the medical staff. There was no distinction between day and night; the room was shrouded in a perpetual dim gray light. Visitors were limited to a handful of immediate family. When we spoke, it was only in hushed tones. I insisted that any discussions of his status or concerns be reserved for hallway conversations.

Somewhere along the way, I'd had enough of the all-consuming, dreary, half-life in that room.

One day, I sprang into action, drew back the drapes, opened the blinds and switched off the hideous overhead UV lights. The gloom instantly dissipated as the sunbeams danced around the room. My heart was lifted immediately. And, although my husband couldn't communicate with words, I believed his heart smiled a little, too.

I came to understand that, while the doctors and staff went about their business, I also had a job to do.

Throughout that week, I executed my own recovery plan. It involved doing things I'm surprised I got away with, but after all, this was New Orleans, where people have warm hearts, great senses of humor and a deep appreciation for the unusual.

Other than family, EJ's two greatest loves were Albert Einstein and Marilyn Monroe. What a terrific combination: science and sex appeal!

I brought their life-sized, standing cutouts into the room and strategically moved them around on a daily basis. The nurses often joined in on the fun and frequently acted as if they were startled by Albert and Marilyn. Sometimes the staff scolded me about these unapproved visitors. Other times, they'd greet them or pretend to have conversations with them.

Soon, the ever-present Albert and Marilyn were a source of great amusement for everyone who came into the room and many others who paused in the hallway for a peek at these famous visitors.

Although he couldn't comment, I'm convinced their laughs and comments had a good effect on EJ.

Cell phones and other electronic devices didn't exist in the early 1990s as they do today. Instead, I used the most advanced level of electronic devices available at the time—cassette tapes, a tape recorder, and headphones—to provide my husband with his favorite classic rock and jazz music. I'm not even sure what a theoretical physicist is, but EJ revered one named Richard Feynman. So, I added Feynman's lectures on tape to his daily listening program and had his books nearby.

Above his bed, I placed the sign:

> Reminder: I can hear everything you say,
> and I have a GREAT memory.
> So, make it GOOOD!

I covered every surface I could with something that had meaning or brought joy to him.

EJ's side of the shared room soon became cluttered with bright and cheerful objects. Get well cards, signed photos from some of the astronauts and pictures of the Three Stooges (more of his favorite heroes) were soon plastered all over the walls and furniture.

One day, while reaching for a pen that had rolled under the bed, I was horrified to discover an old, moldy ice cream cup and dried blood stains under EJ's bed. I looked around the room with a more critical eye than I had before. I realized that it too was unacceptable, and I immediately went to the nurses' station to voice my concerns.

Upon returning to the room, I grabbed my trusty legal pad and formulated my next list of priorities.

Although the room was deep cleaned by my visit the next day, I never wholly trusted the work of any cleaning staff again. With each visit, I brought my own cleaning supplies, including disposable gloves. I didn't do floors, but every other surface from bed tray to bathroom sink got a thorough scrub down and finished off with a heavy dose of disinfectant spray.

Who can say if my actions made a difference in my husband's welfare or comfort? But I also think of it this way: who can say they didn't make a difference for him?

What I am sure of is, although I had no caregiver experience and limited knowledge, I did everything I could think of to support my husband's healing. I chose to go with the philosophy "if there's a remote chance of something making a difference, I'm doing it."

I'm sure I could have done a better job in several areas, but I did my best.

That's all we can do; don't you agree?

STEPPINGSTONES

- ∞ I am now an activist for my husband's care and well-being!

- ∞ It's not important that I know it all; it's important that I give it my all.

- ∞ Bring in the light and the joy! Make it right, no matter the situation.

- ∞ Don't let the current circumstances cause me to forget to express who we really are.

- ∞ By definition, trial and error means I'm going to get it wrong sometimes. My job is to try to maintain the right balance between the two and learn from any mistakes.

- ∞ Always check under the bed for surprises!

CHAPTER 6

Hospital Essentials Go-Kit and Self-Care Kit

He who wishes to secure the good of others has already secured his own.
- Confucius

For every minute spent organizing, an hour is earned.
- Benjamin Franklin

Start where you are. Use what you have. Do what you can.
- Arthur Ashe

Every moment is precious to a caregiver.

My time was primarily focused on healing and nurturing activities for my loved ones and, eventually, myself. The less time I spent scrambling for documents or other needed items, the better. Although I wasn't in control of these new circumstances in our lives, I learned I could often be in control of how I responded to them.

Our family and I spent a great deal of time at EJ's bedside. Eventually, I learned how to efficiently prepare for these situations and provide a greater degree of comfort for my family, throughout these trying times.

The Essentials Go-Kit Checklist was created so I or someone else could "grab and go" essential documents and aids in an emergency or the increasingly routine vigils at the hospital.

Essentials Go-Kit Checklist

It's very helpful to maintain both electronic and hard copies of relevant documents to give to the medical personnel and administrators. These include the following:

- [ ] A master set of documents including copies of all critical insurance cards, relevant legal documents, ID cards, etc.
- [ ] If applicable, a master set copies of relevant military information, DD214, disability rating document, etc.
- [ ] Additionally, some administrators will want to retain copies so have on hand at least one additional set of the above documents.

As with your master set, keep these multiple packets in protective envelopes. Gallon-size storage bags and markers soon became my best friends. These enabled me to keep documents organized and the medications in one place. While you never know when you'll be asked to provide a copy, you can count that it will happen multiple times. Many times, their requests made no sense to me, but my opinions didn't really matter to the administrators.

Just give them what they ask for and move on to more important matters, like spending time with the people you love.

☐ Bag up all medications and prescriptions and have them with you whenever you're at the hospital.

☐ Update all contact information concerning medical providers, family, and closest friends. Have it with you at all times.

If you are a caregiver, you're probably not thinking of your own well-being at this point. However, you need to be prepared to keep yourself strong spiritually, physically and mentally.

You have permission to care for yourself, and in fact, you must be in charge of your own well-being, especially during those long, frequent hospital visits. If you still struggle with taking the time or expending the effort to care for yourself, think about the directions flight attendants give us: place your own oxygen mask on, before assisting others.

If for no other reason, do it for your loved ones.

Self-Care Kit

It's time to create a Self-Care Kit. It may be helpful to think about this as if you were going on a long road trip, with only a few convenience stops along the way. Ask yourself, "What do I need to be comfortable, communicate with others and stay healthy?"

Your Self-Care Kit will probably include many of the items from the list below. Some of these suggestions may not appeal to you or seem necessary but trust me on this . . . the hospital cafeteria and vending machines may not always be available or have something you want to eat. After all, you can only live on stale, fatty chemical-laden snacks and old coffee for so long. You'll also be glad to have that neck pillow and throw blanket after sleeping in the bedside chair for a few nights.

- ☐ Charger(s) for your electronic devices. It's a good idea to have two--one for your phone, another for a tablet or to share with others visiting your loved one. Inevitably, we all needed chargers at the same time.

- ☐ Hard copy of your contacts list. This enables you to accept the help of someone else to contact people while you're occupied with more pressing matters.

- ☐ Neck/travel pillow

- ☐ Light sweater, small throw, or wrap

- ☐ Dry snacks/bars

- ☐ Fresh fruit

- ☐ Gum/mints

- ☐ Protein bars or individual peanut butter or tuna/cracker kits or etc.

- ☐ Bottled water/beverages/powdered instant drink mixes . . . just a couple should do it and may make the difference in getting you through a long night.

- ☐ Tea bags/hot cocoa packets and sweetener if you like it in your tea. I couldn't always get coffee or other beverages, but I could always get hot water to make a cup of tea. Having your own mug is also a good option. Who likes disposable cups, anyway?

- ☐ Exercise/resistance bands. Those stretchy, weigh - nothing, easy to pack, oversized ribbon looking things are very helpful when you need to stretch and move around a bit.

- ☐ Reading materials/eReader. You'll need quiet time and relief from the endless reruns and infomercials that plague hospital TV channels.

- ☐ My set of books include the Bible and other spiritually focused publications. You may have similar items to provide inspiration, comfort, and guidance. If so, these are must-haves in your Self-Care Kit. If you don't have any of these types of publications, now's a great time to start exploring the internet or browsing the hospital gift shop collections for inspiration.

- ☐ Also, consider adding to your self-care kit other types of books you'll enjoy and haven't had the time to read before.

- ☐ Socks, whether you normally wear them or not, you'll want to have something on your feet when you take your shoes off to rest. In New Orleans, I opted to trash my socks after wearing them in the hospital room rather than take them home to launder. You'll need to judge the current hygiene conditions of the patient's room for yourself.

- ☐ Small personal care items such as travel size toothpaste/brush, mouthwash, lotion etc.

- ☐ Whatever personal makeup, hair or cleansing products that will help you stay refreshed. It might be a good time to try dry shampoo. It's a good way for both you and your loved one to stay a little fresher for a little longer. Several excellent choices are usually available in larger grocery or discount stores.

❐ Personal change of clothes and grooming items. You never know when you may end up spending the night or a few days by your loved one's side.

Apps are now available to help you track your checklists and keep them updated. However, I still choose to use old-school legal notepads; it's my thing.

Remember, don't make this overly complicated. Preparing these kits isn't a test of your levels of brilliance, clairvoyance, or performance as a caregiver. The goal is to simply make your life easier and a little more bearable whenever you can. If you don't overdo it, the documents, bag of prescriptions and your Self-Care Kit can easily fit in one tote bag.

Let me say it again, taking care of yourself is also taking care of others.

You will figure out what works best for you and yours. You always do.

STEPPINGSTONES

∽ I may not be able to control what's happening, but I can take charge of this little corner of my world.

∽ Even the most basic organization makes a big difference in my life.

∽ By taking care of myself, I can better take care of others.

∽ Keep it simple; my "Go Kits" are only meant to help me. They are not to become an added burden or another job. It's not a crisis, a failure, or a sign of my inadequacies if I forget something or don't foresee a need. Next time, I can just change the kit, as needed.

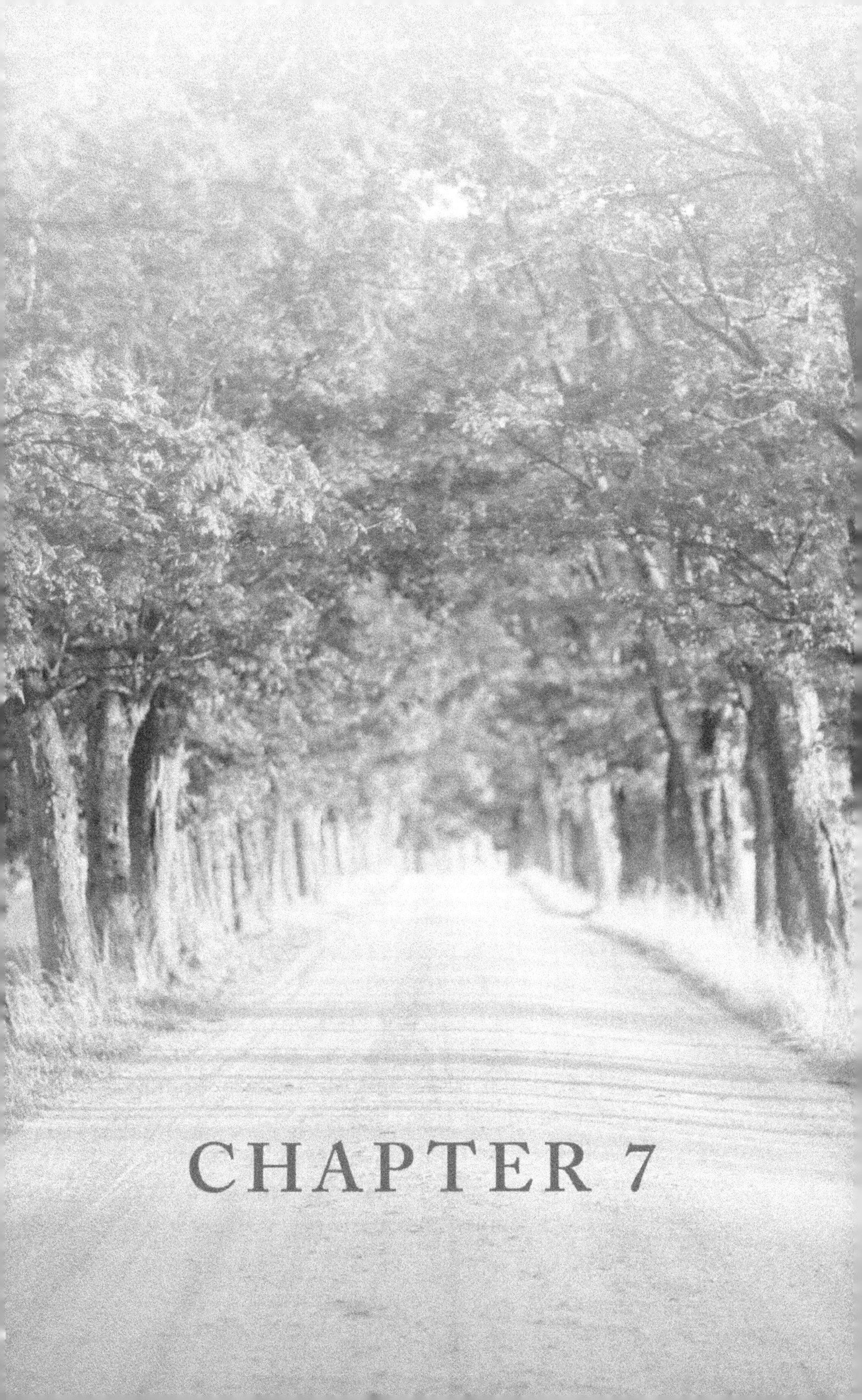

CHAPTER 7

The Kindness of Others

Whatever blesses one, blesses all.
- Mary Baker Eddy

No one has ever become poor by giving.
- Anne Frank

*It's not how much we give but how much love
we put into giving.*
- Mother Teresa

How do I love thee? Let me count the ways.
- Elizabeth Barrett Browning

Kindness is self-perpetuating; it grows and continues to bless yourself and others, over and over again.

Somehow, truly kind people always find a way to lighten the burdens of others. They may be family, friends, neighbors, strangers, administrators, doctors or others. You may not recognize their simple acts of generosity, until some later point in time. Or you may be instantly aware you've been touched by an angel; someone who foresaw a need and acted upon it. Perhaps you have encountered someone who demonstrated selfless love in a thousand little ways yet made a great impact, particularly when you needed it most.

Growing up, I don't recall our family ever having an occasion when we needed the support and encouragement of others outside our immediate circle. As a result, other than prayer, I hadn't experienced the many ways others might express their care and concern.

I don't think I could have survived those first days without the very real kindnesses others showed me and my family. I'm particularly grateful for those neighbors and friends who listened to me without probing for details, judging the situation, or giving too much advice about what they would do in a similar circumstance. I simply wasn't yet ready for anything beyond just trying to cope with each new day.

Throughout the first several months of my husband's hospitalization, here are some of the much appreciated, practical things that others provided for us:

- Pizza and other food treats/deliveries
- Casseroles in the freezer
- Housekeeper arranged dates/prepaid services
- Laundry service arranged dates/prepaid
- Yard mowed
- Trash cans taken out/in
- Cars washed
- Rides to and from school for my son
- Including my son in another family's outings or events
- Gift certificates at a day spa, good for one year

- Receiving mail or packages for me
- Mobile grooming for pets
- In lieu of flowers, specialty food and care baskets delivered straight to the hospital room
- And so much more

At first, I was a little puzzled by these quiet, often anonymous acts of charity. I had never experienced anything like it before and certainly not over such an extended period of time. Not only did I have a deep appreciation for these thoughtful kindnesses, but I also learned from them.

Both of our employers and teammates were very generous and thoughtful, going far beyond any formal guidelines governing these circumstances. We were granted all the time we needed, assistance with benefit processes and ongoing support in a variety of ways.

On a continuing basis, they helped us whenever they could and sometimes in very creative ways.

One of my most memorable events occurred years after EJ's initial medical event, while I was out of state at a corporate conference. I received an early morning call from the overnight caregiver who I had engaged to stay with my husband. She informed me EJ had fallen twice during the night. The EMTs said they had no choice after the second call, and they took him to the hospital for further evaluation. EJ was still being held in the emergency room, and there were no further updates. I assured her that, of course, I would be returning home at once. I immediately notified my direct supervisor of the situation.

As I sat in my hotel room trying to collect my thoughts, there was a sudden, loud knock at my door. It was my boss, who I'd spoken with just moments before, accompanied by another colleague.

She explained that there was no time to spare; I had a first-class ticket for a direct flight home. We had a very short time frame to make the flight. They helped me pack my bags. I didn't even have time to be embarrassed as one of them grabbed my worn "dainties" and nightgown from the chair next to the bed and stuffed them in my suitcase. I was hustled to a waiting car, and to my surprise, they jumped in alongside me. En route to the airport, my boss comforted me and assured me that my husband and I were being held tightly in prayer. She also explained that everything was arranged at the company's expense. My mind swirled as I was quite literally being driven out of town.

The ticket counter agent's eyes nearly popped out of his head when he overheard my boss sternly instructing me, "Do not even think about coming back here, no matter what happens."

I think he misunderstood why the two women were there to ensure I made my flight.

Once on the plane, I barely had time to catch my breath and process everything that had happened that morning. It was a short trip, and it wasn't long before I was back at my husband's bedside.

Certainly, not everyone has the economic resources to arrange for flights and other expensive items for someone else. But for me, the takeaway from that experience was we can all demonstrate the high level of personal concern for someone in need and offer the level of engagement that I experienced.

We should do what we can, whenever we can, to assist with another's need. Truly kind people do this instinctively, without hesitation or calculation; how blessed I am to have so many of these in my life!

We received these and so many other acts of kindness throughout the years. From the small gestures, like sitting and quietly sharing a cup of tea, to much grander actions, I cannot measure the real and positive differences they made in our lives.

I will be forever humbled and grateful for the unexpected support we have received from those who could have easily stated, "I'm sorry, that's all the policy will allow" or "I wish I could help, but..."

Now, when I see another's need and don't know what to do, I ask myself, *what would a nice person do?* or *WWNPD?* It still makes me laugh and reminds me of an important distinction.

While I am nice, I don't always readily come up with an idea on how best to help or thank someone else. However, as I recall my experiences as a receiver of good deeds, I usually find inspiration on how to express my support in a way the other person will appreciate.

My hope is that the gift or action blesses the receiver as I am blessed by giving.

Expressing Gratitude

I can no other answer make,
but thanks, and thanks.
- William Shakespeare

Unselfish acts are the real miracles out of which
all the reported miracles grow.
- Ralph Waldo Emerson

You give much and know not that you give at all.
- Kahlil Gibran

A simple, sincere, and timely "thank you" is the best gift you can bestow upon others who have, in whatever form, made an effort to let you know they care about you. There are some practical ways to accomplish this, even when the majority of your energy and time is focused on your loved one and your family.

I wasn't prepared for the outpouring of support we received, so it's understandable that I also wasn't prepared to express my gratitude for those kindnesses. It was already very hard to keep up with the daily demands in our lives; whenever I thought about saying thank you, I experienced regret at not having done it sooner. Eventually, I figured it out and got it right, or at least I hope so.

Here are some ideas I wish I'd taken advantage of much sooner.

- Purchase packages of thank you notecards or let a friend pick up them up for you. They are inexpensive and readily available, even in grocery stores. Ones that are blank on the inside are nice, but it's easier to complete ones that already include a simple message. You just need to add the recipient's name and sign with a personalized closing.

- Keep an adequate supply of stamps handy.

- Add the thank you notecards to your Hospital Go Kit. You can complete them during those long visits when your loved one is sleeping or out of the room. Also, it's wonderful to have them handy in real-time to thank those at the facility you wish to know how much you appreciate them. This may include cleaning staff, aides, or medical personnel. Your simple expression of gratitude will mean a great deal to them.

- Keep your messages simple. Do not burden yourself unnecessarily by trying to be as poetic as a commercial greeting card. Your personal note is enough to amply convey your gratitude and will be appreciated for its sincerity alone.

- Remember the close friend who asked you to "Please let me know if I can help in any way." It may be time to consider letting that someone help you with the thank you notes. In my opinion, you should always be the one to sign them, but it's a big help to let someone else keep track of what's needed and prepare the cards for you. It's also a big help to have them take care of the mailing of the notes.

Caregivers often come into their new role feeling totally unprepared for their responsibilities; I often had that feeling. I gained more confidence along the way but never really got rid of the sense that I needed to learn more, do more, and give more.

Here are some additional thoughts about the importance of giving that I found very helpful, especially when I was feeling defeated and depleted.

Freely you have received, freely give. Matthew 10:8

God loves a cheerful giver, one who gives without thought of what their reward may be. 2 Corinthians. 9:7

Blessed is that man who sees his brother's need and supplies it, seeking his own in another's good. - Mary Baker Eddy

See first that you yourself deserve to be a giver and an instrument of giving. - Kahlil Gibran

Some people strengthen our society just by being the kind of people they are. - John Gardner

The people who make the difference are not the ones with the credentials, but the ones with the concern. - Max Lucado

Thoroughly, thoroughly, thank you.
- Notecard sentiment in a London shop

The smallest act of kindness is worth more than the grandest intention. - Oscar Wilde

The effect of one good-hearted person is incalculable. - Oscar Arias

We must find time to stop and thank the people who make a difference in our lives. - John Fitzgerald Kennedy

The best way to cheer yourself up is to try to cheer somebody else up. - Mark Twain

If I summon up those memories that have left with me an enduring savor, if I draw up the balance sheet of the hours in my life that have truly counted , surely, I find only those that no wealth could have procured me. - Antoine de Saint-Exupéry

STEPPINGSTONES

∾ Love is the never-ending supply that, when shared freely with others, makes it all work. It's the oil in the machine that blesses us all.

∾ WWNPD makes me laugh at myself and helps me choose the right words and actions when I'm not sure how to respond to someone or a situation. It's okay that I sometimes need this prompter.

∾ Never forget to express my gratitude for the multiple kindnesses we have received.

∾ Remember always how these generous acts had a profound impact on our lives and give as freely to others whenever there is an opportunity or a need.

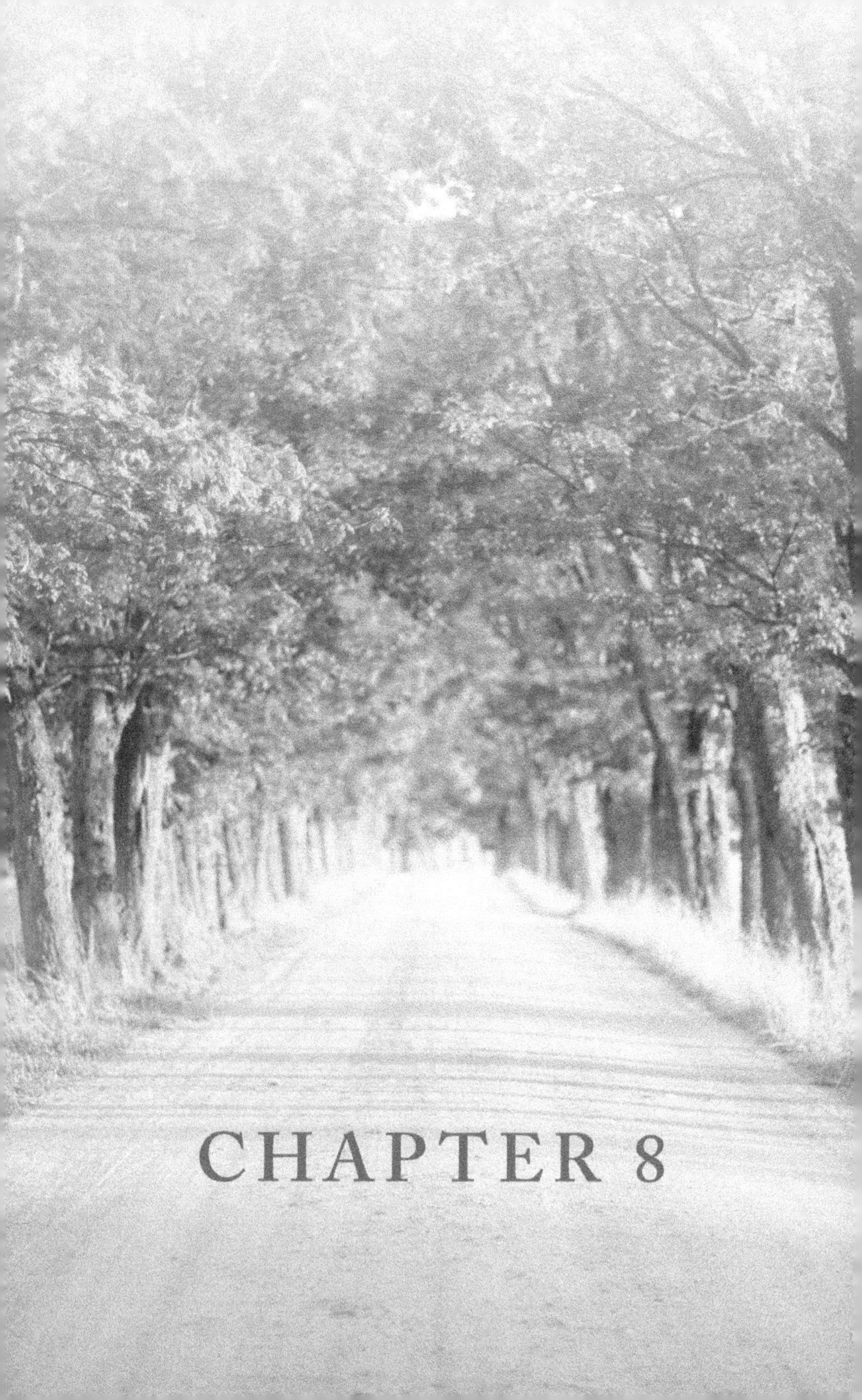

CHAPTER 8

Taking Care of Business

You can't go back and change the beginnings, but
you can start right where you are
and change the ending.
- C.S. Lewis

Realize how good you really are.
- Og Mandio

Prior to his critical medical event, my husband and I were young and healthy. We gave very little thought to Depressing Big Life Questions or comprehensive benefit plans. Although important, we thought that only older people needed to worry about these issues.

We were wrong.

If you haven't done so already, it is time to get your legal/administrative house in order and do it QUICKLY.

At the very time I needed my husband to help make critical decisions and provide background information about our finances, he was no longer mentally available.

I was on my own, frightened, exhausted, and angry to be in this position. Worse yet, when I realized how angry I was with my husband, I felt deep regret at my unfairness. This emotional cycle seemed never-ending.

I thought I was losing my mind.

Although you may find general information about common legal documents from several sources, a word to the wise: lawyers aren't just for rich people or old people or already sick people. There are times and life events in which we all need the guidance of an impartial, experienced professional.

State laws vary and their nuances may be hard to understand. Your brother-in-law's or best friend's situations are not the same as yours, and NO, internet searching for forms is not the best way to protect you and your loved ones from financial disaster or family strife.

Hopefully, you will work with a reputable, family-planning lawyer in advance of a medical event or other change in the family. Having a plan is a great kindness to yourself and to those you love. Otherwise, matters may not be fulfilled as you wish and result in very serious financial issues.

Now is the time to resolve any pending family business matters.

You can do this, and here's how.

Hospitalization

The documents required of the caregiver will vary by state and the medical condition of the patient. At a minimum, you will need to provide the following for the patient:

☐ Insurance coverage information and copies of benefit cards

☐ Personal and family medical history/issues

☐ Primary care provider contact information

☐ List of medications

☐ Personal information: birthdate, social security, etc.

☐ HIPAA (Health Insurance Portability and Accountability Act) Release explains the patient's rights for privacy and will require the patient to provide a list of individuals authorized to receive that information. This form is also where the patient lists those individuals with visitation rights.

☐ Organ donation preference

☐ Work-related injury information, if applicable

☐ Any applicable military/veteran benefit information

Additionally, it's a big advantage to work with a lawyer in advance of your actual need to prepare the following:

- ❐ Medical directives
- ❐ Powers of attorney for both medical and financial issues
- ❐ Advance Health Care Directive
- ❐ Living Will
- ❐ Will(s)
- ❐ Trust
- ❐ Special Needs Trust, if applicable
- ❐ Comprehensive Kids' Protection Planning
- ❐ Comprehensive Elder/Disability Protection Plan
- ❐ Disposition of Remains

I don't know why we didn't handle these things in advance.

Perhaps they seemed too depressing at the time. However, it was much worse for me to have to deal with them all on my own, while in the middle of a crisis. Once these matters were settled, I actually gained a great sense of peace. It was comforting to have the decisions on delicate matters completed; I didn't have to think about them anymore. My children also expressed their gratitude that, on my behalf, they would never have to deal with these difficult issues on their own.

Also, I couldn't have anticipated the multiple times throughout the years my husband would be readmitted to a hospital or transferred to a different care facility.

Each time, I needed to provide many of the same documents at the time of his admission to the new facility. Having everything organized enabled me to provide the needed documents without delay or additional stress.

Once I made the necessary decisions and implemented my recordkeeping system, it was a great relief not to have to make tough choices or chase down documents in the midst of dealing with my husband's health crisis.

What the Nurses and Administrators Need You to Know

- Records needed for admission may vary by state. Trust them to lead you through what's needed for the current circumstances.

- Be sure that the HIPAA form is updated. One of its purposes is to identify who is authorized to receive medical information concerning the patient. The staff is required by law to comply with this document and will not be able to make exceptions.

- The doctor alone is authorized to share medical results or other information with you or others. This includes lab results, X-rays, diagnostic testing, etc. Only a doctor may interpret and discuss these items with the appropriate person. Do not become frustrated or angry when someone tells you that they cannot speak with you on a given topic; the doctor is the only one who can give you the information you seek. They are giving you the right answer.

Communicating
with Employers

It's also likely that you will need to communicate with at least one employer about the recent medically related events.

Before you do, please heed these words of caution, coming from a Human Resources executive with more than thirty years of experience in the field.

However sincerely concerned the employer may be about you or your loved one's welfare, their job is to plan how best to address the absence of their valued employee. This entails getting as much information as they need to make decisions about the current and future probability of your or your loved one's employment status.

Be honest and timely with the information you share with the appropriate representatives of the employer. This includes human resources and insurance representatives. That said, do not go into unnecessary or too much detail regarding the injury or illness, your hopes, or your fears. If you talk too much or send documents with more information than has been requested, you will only raise more questions and potentially complicate matters.

We're all very much like the jury who is told to "disregard earlier statements." We cannot "unhear" things that have been said. The same is true for your employer and benefit providers.

If you are unfocused or provide too much background information, you complicate things that the employer is attempting to understand. It's not helpful and may be quite confusing. This can result in a delay in processing benefits, scheduling a return to work and other items.

Additionally, and depending upon the size of the organization, do not share anything related to the patient's medical condition or return to work status with anyone outside of Human Resources. This includes managers, coworkers and vendors or anyone else with a connection to the employer.

There's a very good reason for this advice.

Remember the child's game "Telephone"? Even the best-intentioned people mix up information when passing it along. It's best that you remain the single, controlled source of anything related to your loved one's health and benefit status when dealing with employers. Additionally, do you really want to contribute to gossip or speculation about your loved one and family? Instead, exercise discretion and good judgment at all times.

You should consider your conversations with the employer to be critical business conversations, and therefore, you must take precise notes including who you spoke with, the date, the main points of the conversation and any pending action items.

We'll cover more about the importance of communication and recordkeeping, later.

Here are things that the employer should know:

- Date of event/admission

- Expected date of release and projected dates of absence from the workplace. It's okay to say, "I don't know at this time."

- Best way to contact you. Confirm that all information on file is correct.

- If the patient will be returning to work, the employer will also need:

- Release date to return to work and whether it's a full or partial release.

- Any restrictions concerning work-related activities or hours.

Here are things you should know:

- FMLA (Family Medical Leave Act) currently provides up to twelve workweeks of leave in a twelve-month period, for eligible employees. According to dol.gov, FMLA leave is available to qualified employees for:

  o The birth of a child and to care for the newborn child within one year of birth;

  o The placement with the employee of a child for adoption or foster care and to care for the newly placed child within one year of placement;

  o To care for the employee's spouse, child, or parent who has a serious health condition;

  o A serious health condition that makes the employee unable to perform the essential functions of his or her job;

- Any qualifying exigency arising out of the fact that the employee's spouse, son, daughter, or parent is a covered military member on "covered active duty;" or

- Twenty-six workweeks of leave during a single twelve-month period to care for a covered servicemember with a serious injury or illness if the eligible employee is the servicemember's spouse, son, daughter, parent, or next of kin (military caregiver leave)

- The guidelines regarding the FMLA approval process include strict timelines and needed certifications. Additionally, employers may establish their own policies governing the application of any available leave time (sick days, PTO, vacation, etc.) in coordination with FMLA. As these policies vary between employers, be sure that you understand how they apply to your situation.

- HIPAA, amongst other provisions, protects the patient's rights concerning privacy of medical information and other insurance factors.

Take a deep breath; the FMLA and HIPPA may sound scary at first, but once you begin to read the information, they're not as hard to understand as you may have imagined. The forms for FMLA are simple to follow. Also, the patient's doctor should be very familiar with the requirements of HIPAA and be able to help you navigate through the process and forms.

What's important is that you understand these federal laws protect privacy and provide benefits to the employee. Therefore, no matter how hard they may probe or ask open-ended questions, you should offer your employer no more information than what is required by law.

That's not an adversarial position; it's a wise one.

Additionally, you should ask for written confirmation of the following:

- Any available paid time off, sick pay, vacation, or other benefit days available to the employee
- All other benefit plans in which the employee is currently enrolled.
- Insurance benefits company's contact information, plan/policy numbers and their claims process and timelines.
- What forms, if any, are required and who needs to sign them? When do they need to be returned?

The benefit plans may include medical coverage, short-term and long-term disability, life insurance, and any supplemental plans. Depending on the employment conditions, there may also be specific plans to cover expat situations, out-of-state coverage/treatment, etc.

Insurance programs have very strict enrollment requirements and deadlines. The proper information must be completed and submitted per the requirements of the plan.

Unfortunately, many employees don't respond in a timely way or provide the needed information to complete the enrollment process. Far too many times, I've had to share with families the heartbreaking news that their loved one didn't enroll in coverage that was offered and available to them. Consequently, the families had to deal with the devastating financial issues they hadn't anticipated.

Don't assume anything; ensure all dependents, beneficiaries and their contact information are updated.

I have first-hand knowledge of a case involving an employee's passing. He had divorced and remarried many years before his death. During their twelve-year marriage, he and his second wife raised a family together. Unfortunately, in all that time the employee never updated his beneficiary designation on his life insurance policy. Although there had been great friction between them for years, upon his death, the ex-wife received the substantial life insurance payout. The current wife and children got nothing.

Money Matters

Prior to marrying EJ, I'd been a divorced, single mom of three. It was a Herculean effort for me to provide financially for our family during those years. Although I worked three jobs—one full-time and two part-time—we just squeaked by each month.

Everything was a struggle.

We often had oatmeal for dinner, as was the case on one particular night. As we ate, I asked the children what they learned in school that day. One of them answered they learned about people in the olden days called peasants. The peasants were so poor, they had to eat something called gruel, if they had anything to eat at all. Then came the surprisingly tough question.

"Mommy, what is gruel?"

"It's a sort of soup made out of oatmeal," I answered without much thought. Immediately and in unison, both Lynn and Tommy silently looked down at their dinner bowls. They appeared quite distressed and the expressions on their faces let me know they were very concerned that we too were poor peasants.

Johnny was so young, he just kept munching away without a care.

"No, no, no, their gruel wasn't the same as our oat-meal. We have milk and brown sugar. Oh, and cinnamon too. I promise you, they're different; I just didn't explain it the right way, and besides, we like oatmeal, don't we?"

"I LIKE oatmeal!" three-year-old Johnny gave out a cheer, as he waved his spoon high in the air, while remnants of sticky, sweet globs of oatmeal dripped off his chin. Sarah, our amiable St. Bernard, rested patiently next to his chair, clearly hoping to get to Johnny before I could wash his face.

We all laughed and went back to finishing our hot, satisfying, dinner of the world's most appreciated bowls of oatmeal.

However, the laughter never seemed to last as long as my worries for us.

I spent sleepless nights wondering how I could spread my paycheck far enough to cover childcare, mortgage, food, and other necessities. I always paid my bills, but I couldn't always pay them on time. So, it wasn't unusual to get home late at night after picking up the kids to find that one or more of the basic utilities had been cut off.

"Surprise! We're going camping tonight," I'd say to the kids, in my best attempt at a cheerful voice. I was as prepared as I could be to get us through those increasingly frequent nights without power or water. A candle and matches were kept near the door, a pitcher of water in the refrigerator and powdered milk, Cheerios, peanut butter, jelly, and bread in the cupboard, ensuring we could make it at least a couple of days, if needed.

I hated that my children had to experience those days.

My parents, who lived only two blocks away, were aware that things were tight but had no idea how deep my money concerns really were. It wasn't their fault; I'd done everything I could to conceal the truth from them. I knew they weren't in a position to help financially and didn't want them to experience any additional anxiety due to my situation.

Unexpectedly, my carefully guarded secret was exposed one night during a family dinner at their home. Within a few moments after he'd excused himself from the table to use the restroom, young Tommy loudly sounded an alarm.

"Oh, no! Now we have to go camping at Grandma's house *too!*"

We all looked up in shock and confusion. As mothers always do, I rushed to help him and discover the source of his distress. The others followed close behind me.

Although Tommy repeatedly flipped the light switch, the bathroom remained completely dark. Realizing the truth, for once I became the bearer of good news; the cause of his anxiety was simply a burned-out light bulb. As the bulb was quickly replaced, Tommy's despair at the thought of "going camping" at his grandparents' home evaporated.

When we returned to the dinner table, my parents demanded to know what was meant by "going camping." The children each hurriedly tumbled out their versions of the details of our lives. Honestly, their stories weren't as depressing as the real facts were. But they were enough to trouble my parents despite my ongoing protestations that we would be fine.

A few years later I remarried, and EJ provided well for us. Although we had a comfortable lifestyle, I opted to continue working. I enjoyed my work, and as an added bonus at this point in my career, I was earning quite a substantial income. In fact, I soon earned more than

EJ. Somehow it doesn't seem fair that brilliant scientists and educators are paid less than other professionals, but that's the way of the world— at least for now.

I appreciated that my husband handled all financial matters and thought it a blessing not to have to personally deal with banks and bills anymore. I resisted my husband's attempts to educate me about our accounts, debts, and investments. I considered it a luxury to no longer need to think about any money matters.

I was wrong.

Our credit score went from excellent to dismal within the first six months following my husband's massive stroke. This was entirely my fault due to my lack of knowledge and prior avoidance of being involved in our finances, even at the most basic level.

It's hard to remember the days before iPhones or other electronic devices, but at that time, everything was done by hard copy. It wasn't long before the mail piled up and often went unanswered while I tried to balance maintaining daily hospital visits, working, taking care of the family, providing updates to everyone on my husband's condition and so much more. I had no idea what our bills were or where he kept our financial records.

I was always behind and began getting a lot of collection calls from bill collectors. My stress was growing like a big, nasty hairball and it—in addition to everything else going on at the time—took a heavy toll on my well-being.

You can avoid this.

Here are some of the things you should know or be able to quickly locate, regarding your family finances:

☐ All passwords, account/policy numbers, contact information and beneficiaries.

- Assets

  o General understanding of any assets including real estate, vehicles, jewelry, collections, antiques and other items of value

☐ Banking/Investments

- Savings &/or checking
- Routing number
- Account number
- Joint or single account
- Beneficiary
- Online password
- ATM password
- Balances
- Auto deposits and dates
- Auto debits and dates
- Safety deposit box access
- Investment accounts; all relevant contact information, account information/balances, beneficiary

☐ Financial obligations/Recurring bills

- Mortgage or rent

  o Lender contact info/loan number
  o Who is on the mortgage? Is it jointly or singly held?

- o Terms of the mortgage
- o Payment amount/due date
- o Any second mortgage
- o Balances

- Car payments

  - o Lender/loan number
  - o Payment amount/due date
  - o Who is on the loan? Is it a joint or single loan?
  - o Balance

- Credit Cards

  - o Account numbers
  - o Joint or single accounts
  - o Balance
  - o Payment information

- Utilities

  - o Service providers
  - o Account numbers
  - o Due dates
  - o Whose name is on the account? This really matters in some states. For example, I had a very difficult time proving my residency status in Louisiana, the only state under the Napoleonic Code, because of this very issue.

- Phone

- o Service provider
- o Payment information
- Alimony or child support
- Other

☐ Pension plans

☐ Annuities/IRAs

☐ Disability insurance, both short and long-term

☐ Life insurance

☐ Home services providers, as applicable. Know contact information, service schedules and fees.

- Yard care
- Trash/recycle
- Septic tank maintenance
- Propane
- Pool maintenance

Whew! Sounds like a lot to handle, but it really isn't *if* you organize things before you need them.

The important thing is that you understand your family finances and know how to access needed updated information and resources (including money) as they are needed.

You can do it!

About Time

"How do you do it? How do you find the time to do it all? What's the secret?" asked my trusted friend, as we shared a heaping plate of nachos during our lunch break from work. He was like a brother to me and, for the most part, knew the real struggles our family was experiencing.

I took a long pause to reflect, and ultimately, for once, I decided to respond truthfully.

"I guess my secret is that I don't even try to do it all anymore. And of those few things I manage to accomplish, I don't do any of them very well. I gave up trying to do everything perfectly a long time ago. And even though I don't like it; I've learned to be okay with that."

"Could've fooled me. I think you're doing an amazing job," he sweetly replied before quickly returning his attention to the dripping nacho in his hand. He was generously refusing to acknowledge—or perhaps because of our friendship, he was blind to—the changes in me. My friend thought I was strong, when in fact, he was unaware I had eventually learned to live with being stretched so thin that I was sometimes at the point of breaking.

Or maybe I was already broken; to be honest, I simply couldn't tell anymore.

* * *

How we referred to time was amongst the many, many changes within our family. Now, almost everything in our lives was categorized as either pre-stroke or post-stroke. Also, the definitions of time measurements became much more fluid for me, as in the phrases "short- term" and "long-term."

Pre-stroke, short-term topics included things like "Where would you like to go for dinner tonight?" or "What are we doing this weekend?" Long-term goals included far-away plans like ultimate professional achievements, once-in-a-lifetime trips and other desired big decisions and experiences.

Post-stroke, the initial short-term goal was simple—that EJ would make it through the night. Later, long- term topics might include a hope that he would survive throughout the next six months or be able to walk with the aid of a walker within the next two years.

Post-stroke, I was swamped with tasks and had no hope of accomplishing them all. I didn't know this was common for caregivers.

Pre-stroke, I thought I was good at multitasking, but post-stroke, I realized there would never be enough time to do things in the way I would normally do them. Since I couldn't control the increasing demands placed upon my time, the only answer was to improve the way I dealt with them.

For the lucky few, knowing how to effectively multi-task is an intuitive skill. However, this wasn't the case for me.

I needed to develop better time management skills.

While I knew that maximizing the management of time is an essential part of taking care of business for you and your loved ones, I didn't really know how to go about making the needed changes to accomplish this. It wasn't easy for me, but a lot of changes in my thinking had to occur before I understood how to use my time more effectively.

As an example, my family, work and financial priorities were continually redefined, and their order of predominance shifted based upon our current experiences and needs. I needed to quickly hone my skills at anticipating, becoming more flexible and reacting accordingly to these changes.

It was a matter of our survival.

Don't sweat the small stuff, I needed to remind myself throughout the post-stroke years. That's far easier said than done, for me. Yet eventually and only by pure necessity, I learned to let go of things that didn't really matter.

Somewhere along the way, I developed a strategy to recover at least some of my wasted and lost time and then reallocate this precious commodity in the ways I chose. I called it "The Pizza Theory of Time."

It works like this . . . think of time as a hot, delicious pizza, with all your favorite toppings. Now, there's a long line of people, projects, and activities before you, and every one of them wants a piece of your pizza. Some even demand it. No matter how generous you are, you only have one, finite-sized pizza.

This is not a "fishes and loaves" story.

First, you have to realize that you are in control of how you share your pizza with others. No matter how compelling their arguments may seem, you alone must decide how your time will be allocated.

This project wants a big slice of your time; this person says they only want a sliver; you enjoy spending time with this one and want to give them a big slice of your time, and so on. There isn't any way for you to divide your pizza equally or to feed them all. You must decide the distinctions between "wants" and "needs," how much you give and who, if anyone, you turn away.

Oh, and if you don't remember to factor your own need for nourishment into the equation, will there be anything left for yourself?

There were some time demands I couldn't adjust; I fulfilled these tasks as required of me. However, there were other activities I could shift around, however reluctant I may be to make the needed changes. I reevaluated the time dedicated to things like familiar, but unnecessary, household routines, leisurely shopping trips, lingering too long with my morning coffee, etc. Making changes in these habits was like mining for gold, timewise. I discovered more time to do what I needed to accomplish without a lot of sacrifice. Conversely, I held tightly to other interests that brought me some respite and happiness if they weren't expensive in the sense of time spent on them.

It took me a little while to figure out how to allocate my "pizza of time" and still have something, if even just a nibble, for myself; but the pay-off was worth it. I got more accomplished and forgave myself for not accomplishing it all.

I'm confident that, if needed, you or the caregiver in your life will be able to find the best ways to capture more time to accomplish those things you desire.

STEPPINGSTONES

∽ Grownups need to understand and take responsibility for their finances.

∽ Don't avoid the administrative stuff I'm not comfortable handling. Instead, anticipate what's needed, prepare, execute (do my job), and keep good records.

∽ Even if I'm not the one paying the bills and managing the money, I need to understand where everything is, what's required to make it all work and what the passwords are.

∽ Now that it's my job to manage our finances, I can set up whatever system for tracking and paying bills works best for me. It can always be switched back on the happy day I'm not in charge of it anymore.

∽ Don't sweat the small stuff; stop being afraid and feeling overwhelmed!

∽ I can do this.

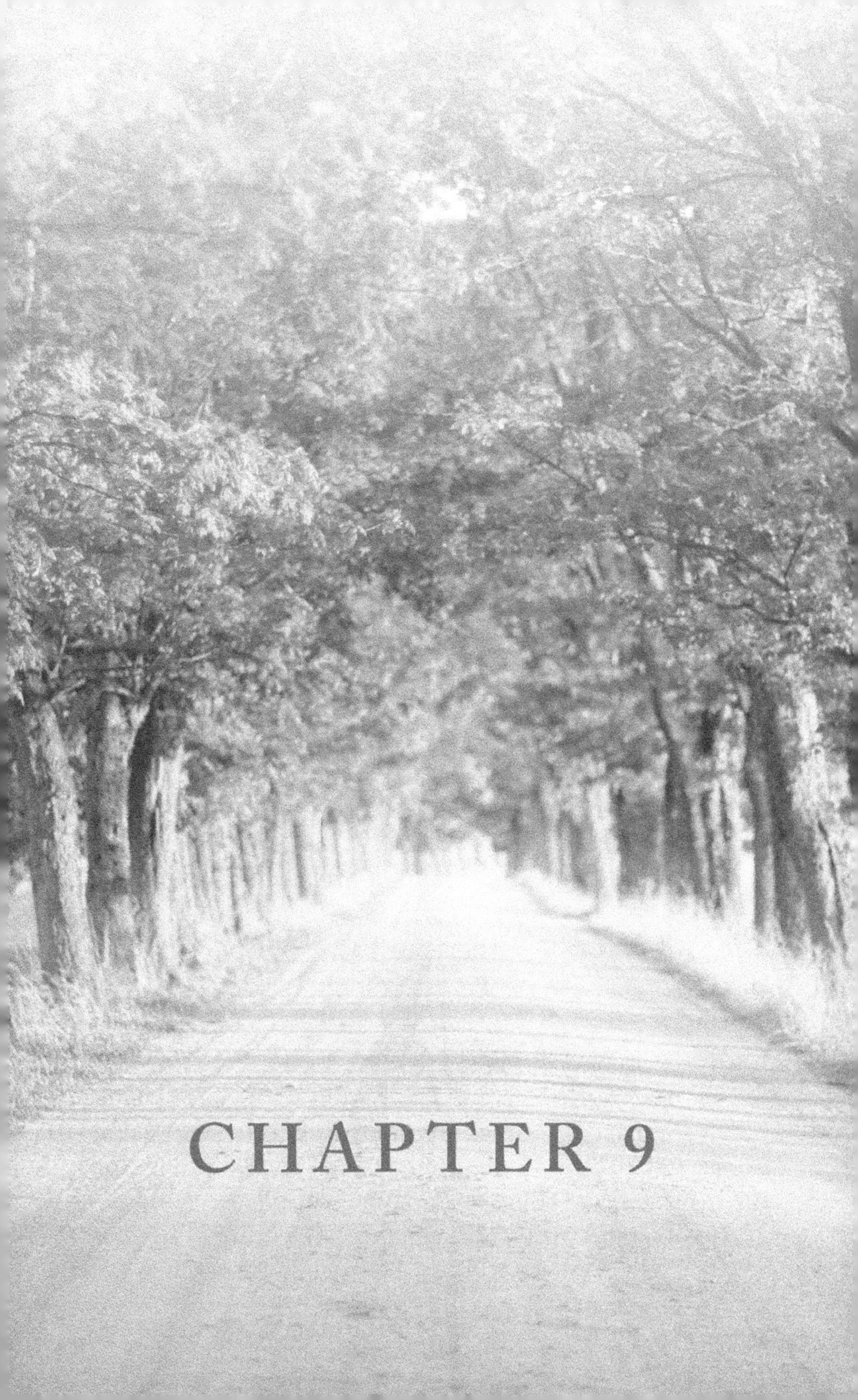

CHAPTER 9

Home at Last, Working with the In-Home Care Team

Never forget that with God all things are possible.
Matthew 19:26

I've got you. Don't be afraid,
for I am with you always. Don't be discouraged,
for I am your God. I will give you
the strength you need and I will uphold you
with the right hand of my righteousness.
That's a forever promise.
Isaiah 41:10

Rejoice in hope; be patient in times of tribulation;
continue to pray constantly.
Romans 12:12

It was several months before EJ was released to come home for the first time. This followed months of care in multiple hospitals and rehabilitation facilities. He was to come home, not because he had recovered, but simply because the insurance coverage for inpatient care had run out.

It was a milestone moment for our family.

Now we were on our own to care for a six-foot-tall, partially paralyzed adult with the mindset of a two- year- old. He needed 24-hour care and assistance with the most basic daily activities. When he wasn't sleeping, EJ was often confused, uncooperative and angry with his new physical and mental limitations. He struggled to speak and was frustrated at not being able to communicate his thoughts and his needs.

It broke my heart.

While I was joyous to have him home again, the responsibilities were daunting. I didn't know if we could handle it, but somehow, we did.

What to Expect from In-Home Therapy Sessions

Initially, we had the in-home support of therapists. As a result of the massive stroke, multiple kinds of therapists were assigned to work with my husband. Although I was confused about their roles at first, I quickly learned their different skills and goals for my husband.

All therapists start with an assessment of the client to establish a baseline and therapy plan. All situations are unique, and they will arrange their visits and session content based upon the individual's needs. They will discuss the recovery plan with you and provide written instructions for exercises to be practiced between visits.

In-home therapy involves a very personal interaction both with the patient and the family members in the home. In my experience, therapists are people who genuinely care about the well-being of others. However, because of the level of personal interaction, sometimes the lines between relationships become blurred.

Most of the therapists we worked with were affable and nice to talk with; it was easy to develop relationships with them. I often thought of them as friends. I looked forward to their regular visits and hoped they would have a little extra time for a short visit with me. However, in retrospect, I could have done a better job of letting them just get on with their work.

I have since learned that therapy is most effective when all parties maintain the appropriate balance in the personal and professional partnership.

While there are areas of overlap between therapists, the physical therapist's (PT) focus is fairly straightforward. He worked with my husband on sitting up, strength and mobility. We didn't see much progress during the early days, but there was a massive improvement over the years.

The speech therapist (ST or SLP, Speech/Language/Pathology) concentrates on helping the patient to understand the meaning of words spoken to them and improve their memory skills. They are concerned with thought organization, cognition and swallowing. As needed, STs also work with patients to improve their verbal and written skills.

Occupational therapy (OT) is very interesting and based upon a holistic approach. These therapists work with patients of all ages to overcome any limiting factors in their daily lives due to illness, injury, or disability. Or more simply, they focus on activities of daily living and interaction within the home environment.

Activities of daily living (ADLS) include the following:

- Ambulating, walking, getting around
- Feeding
- Bathing
- Dressing/Grooming
- Using the toilet
- Continence management
- Getting in/out of a bed or chair

What In-Home Therapists and Care Providers Needed from Me

- Stick to the schedule, as much as possible. Communicate any necessary schedule adjustments ahead of time.

- Have the patient ready for the session before the therapist's arrival.

- Provide a quiet, workable space for the session.

- Share any updates on the patient's condition, reactions following the prior session or other concerns with the therapist.

- Ask questions about exercises/activities.

- In between visits, help the patient stay on schedule with the prescribed exercises/activities.

- Be prepared to observe or participate in the therapy sessions, if requested by the therapist.

- Otherwise, do not hover or interrupt the session.

What I Wanted In-Home Therapists and Care Providers to Know

- Any particular rules of the house, i.e., please remove your shoes at the door, etc.
- Preferred restroom for their use, if needed.
- Any boundaries that might have been or potentially may be crossed. This one's a little difficult to explain, but much like the definition of pornography, "You'll know it when you see it."

Here is one of a variety of incidents, from my personal experience.

One day, while watching TV, I accidentally fell asleep on the sofa. Nick, the physical therapist, was in session with my husband in another room. At some point into their session, I awoke to discover the gentleman with his feet up in the recliner next to me. I had always offered him a cold drink, so I wasn't surprised to see the soda in his hand. However, I was surprised to find the TV had been turned off, and he was simply watching me as I slept.

It was a bit unsettling, an intrusion into my personal space and a private moment.

Most of all, it was just plain creepy.

"Where's my husband?" I asked.

He replied that the session ended early because EJ was very tired and had gone to bed.

"Then we're finished here, right?"

"Yes, Ma'am" were the last words I ever received from him. He quickly got up out of the chair and left our home.

The following day, I contacted his supervisor to discuss the uncomfortable situation. However, before I could explain my concerns, I learned that the therapist had asked to be assigned to another patient, and I was given the name of his replacement.

It was a great solution for all of us.

Here's the bottom line, even though you may not always feel it, you are in charge of your family, your life, and your home. Do not be intimidated by anyone or uncomfortable in addressing issues that matter to you and yours.

I found that the more clarity I provided, the less drama and stress we all experienced.

Selecting Non-Medical Caregivers

My employment outside of the home was critical for our family's financial survival.

At different points in time, I could only fulfill my professional responsibilities with the assistance of an experienced in-home caregiver. You may also find it necessary to engage someone outside of the family to assist with the caregiver role at some point in time.

Be sure to check if financial assistance is available to you before engaging someone. If so, your plan may require specific certifications, etc. It's far better to know any deciding factors required by your plan before you begin the search for an in-home caregiver. In our case, the costs of these services were not covered by insurance or other benefits. This presented a huge, but necessary, financial burden on our family.

You may need help finding in-home assistance. Thankfully today, services and online resources are available to help you make the right caregiver match for your situation. These didn't exist when I needed to hire someone. I relied upon friends and others for their referrals and suggestions. Ultimately, whenever the need arose, I was able to connect with the perfect person to help us.

During the interviewing process, the first meeting was always just between the candidate and me. If we moved forward, the second meeting included my husband and our pets—our sweet pup Moondoggy and monstrously huge ginger cat Ajax. It was essential that we had a good match between each of them.

My initial screening questions included:

☐ What is your experience as a caregiver, including clients with similar conditions?

☐ What is your shift availability, and do you have any scheduling restrictions?

☐ Why did you choose this line of work?

☐ What's important to you in this assignment?

☐ Is there a past situation that made you uncomfortable while caring for someone?

☐ What was the best assignment you ever had and why?

☐ Are you comfortable in a house with pets?

☐ Are you available outside of the regular schedule? Although limited, there will be times when I will be required to travel for work. Are you available for overnights and weekends, if given enough notice?

☐ What are your salary expectations? Is that a flat weekly rate or do you calculate by the hour? If the amount of time varies, that is, if it's a short week, will you charge less? If the time runs over, will you charge more? **NOTE:** here you are simply asking what their expectations are; you are not agreeing to them. I never took advantage of someone who asked for too little. Conversely, I never hired anyone with outrageous demands, even if they eventually agreed to take less. These folks will make up the balance of their desired compensation somehow, and it won't be to the benefit of you or your loved one.

☐ How flexible is your schedule? Although I generally have a set schedule, the nature of my work requires that I be flexible. There will be times that I need to stay later to resolve an issue, and I may only be able to let you know at the last minute. Is that a problem?

☐ Will you please provide references?

I also discussed the very few rules of the house; not smoking indoors was always the first issue we discussed. Additionally, I was very clear that others were not allowed in the home. This meant no visitors, whether or not they were related to the caregiver.

We were able to maintain highly qualified and dedicated partners in my husband's care for years, by sorting out as much "stuff" as possible upfront.

For me, it was also very important to clarify my priorities. I was completely transparent about my expectations, including but not limited to the following:

☐ I began each conversation with, "I'm providing a general overview of my view of the main points of this job. However, things may vary, and if they do, let's both do our best to talk about them in advance."

☐ "My husband's care is my first priority, and I want it to be yours too. He should receive your full attention. I am not asking you to do any housework, laundry, or errands for us," I stated very early in our conversation.

In our home, however, preparing a good lunch and an afternoon snack was part of the gig. I invited them to share the same food and committed to also having some of their favorite treats and beverages on hand for them.

I later learned from those who helped us throughout the years that this is one of the reasons they chose to work with us rather than other employers. They appreciated my personal respect for them and the distinction that they were not there as housekeepers. All the caregivers I hired throughout the years focused on my husband's care, not my household chores.

Conversely, I was equally respectful and clear with anyone coming into my home to help with the house. I honored our agreements, and they understood that they were not expected to assist with my husband's care in any way. I was also transparent about his condition, so that they would not be uncomfortable if he asked questions of them that normally would seem a bit overly familiar or invited them to sit and visit. Everyone that came into our home was very kind and understanding. Many shared with me that they enjoyed EJ's sense of humor and positive outlook on life. I know these interactions made his days brighter, too.

If you are in the position to hire a caregiver for assistance with your loved one, it will be very helpful to keep these lines very clear. If you need assistance with household chores or cooking, you must state that up front.

Only one potential hire as a caregiver turned us down. She was quite tiny and delicate, and her former clients had all been elderly women. She stated that she wasn't prepared to be responsible for a six-foot-tall man with limited mobility.

Although I was disappointed, I appreciated her honesty very much. In the end, she saved us all a lot of time and trouble.

We all have our quirks, and people who come into your home to provide a service are no different than the rest of us. Working as a team, you'll be sharing personal spaces and lots of information. You need to build trust and demonstrate respect for each other as you work together toward your loved one's recovery.

Since you're all in the mix together, let's hope you come up with a happy gumbo!

Some peculiarities you can live with, while others require you to draw a firm line. However, word of caution here, pick your battles carefully; you don't want to lose a good caregiver or damage the relationship over differences that don't really matter.

Celia

Celia, a very kind and attentive caregiver, greeted me each morning with a big smile and a sunny *"Hola!"*

She was a fireball of energy, pausing only for a moment to store her purse on the desk, before heading straight to the kitchen to start her morning routine.

Her habit was to address the kitchen with a deep sigh, as if she'd walked into a teenager's disastrous, smelly bedroom. She'd then grab a broom and begin robustly sweeping the floor.

"Tsk, tsk, tsk, tsk," she loudly repeated the entire time she vigorously attacked the floor. It was more than a little intimidating to watch, as her normally pleasant face became fiercely intense.

I often wondered what that poor floor had done to her to receive such a punishing beating.

At first, I felt embarrassed that, evidently, I did not meet Celia's impeccable housekeeping standards. After a while, I realized no one could say I was a bad housekeeper, and I became puzzled at her approach.

After all, Celia and I had agreed up front that housework wasn't a part of her job and yet, she chose to do that work. I kept up my housework throughout the week and deep-cleaned on Saturdays. Celia never had to deal with dishes or other messes from the night before.

Additionally, all in all, I was considered a fairly tidy person.

I concluded that Celia was either a clean freak or intentionally trying to make me feel inadequate . I knew her to be far too genuine and kind to play mean head games, so I opted for the first choice. I also decided that there are far worse things than having an obsessive, Lover-of-Sweeping in your home.

In fact, it was actually pretty nice.

I never questioned Celia regarding her feelings about the state of the house's cleanliness and after a while, I changed my attitude about her "tsk, tsk, tsk, tsking." Instead of becoming offended or irritated, I began to regard her commentary with affection—just another way Celia attacked her day with diligence and gusto. I eventually realized her enemy was the perceived dust, not me.

Celia cared for my husband for years and was sorely missed when she relocated to join her daughter's family. Although , I do think the floors may have been somewhat grateful of her absence.

Doris

Some behaviors are more serious than quirks, and you'll need to decide if you are willing to accommodate them in your own home or take a stand with the caregiver.

Neither my husband nor I were smokers, and I made it very clear during each interview that our home was a no-smoking space. One dear lady, Doris, committed that she would only smoke outside on the screened-in patio, where the comfortable cafe table and chairs, overlooking a lovely garden, were ready for her use.

Unfortunately, a few months into our agreement, Doris began sneaking smoke breaks in the house. Florida's winter weather is gorgeous, so there was no excuse not to comply with our agreement.

Although she tried to mask the odor, no amount of air freshener could cover up the traces of her deeds. The heavy smoke and cover-up air spray permeated the air and lingered in the furniture. Eventually, I had to have an authentic conversation about it. I had no choice but to ask her directly if she was smoking in the house. Doris firmly denied it and claimed the odor was coming in from the outside. It stopped for a while, but she soon began to smoke inside the house again.

I have a few non-negotiables. Among them, I can't tolerate liars nor someone who disrespects a mutual agreement.

I was sad, but we had to part ways with Doris. She was sad too, but incapable of honoring her word.

Cheryl

Cheryl was the kindest and most efficient caregiver, ever. A petite dynamo, with a no-nonsense attitude and a sarcastic sense of humor, it was immediately clear to me that we'd be a great match. I fully trusted that she could handle anything that might come her way and that EJ was safe in her care.

I was right.

Cheryl was truly a blessing during the many years she was with us. But as sometimes happens even within a family, eventually I needed to address a couple of things that were no-goes for me.

For a long time, I had chosen to ignore that Cheryl had continually changed all the glasses in the cupboard from rim up to rim down.

It was a small thing, a personal preference, a battle not worth picking.

One day, the cat litter box, which was kept in the laundry room and cleaned daily, got moved out to the back porch. In the evening, I moved it back and thought, *I'll have to talk to Cheryl about this.* However, I didn't, and she continued to move it out each day. I meant to speak with her, but something else more important always came up first. I didn't ask her to *not* move the box, and she continued to relocate it daily.

Annoying, but not a deal breaker.

Oftentimes, I was unavoidably delayed in getting home from work. It was simply the nature of my job. While Cheryl and I were always in complete alignment about the handoff of her shift, on these nights, we were both rushed. Consequently, during the changing of the guard, there was no time for us to speak. Cheryl and I had just enough time to wave and say, "Have a good night," as we passed each other. Inside there would be a note from her providing highlights of the day's activities and EJ's condition.

Eventually, I began to notice that, after she left for the day, Cheryl's massive, overstuffed knitting bag remained next to the sofa, plopped open with its colorful contents spilling over the rim. At first, I thought it was an oversight. But later I realized there was a new pattern in our lives; the bag was only left behind on those late nights.

It sounds ridiculous now, but at the time it really annoyed me to come home exhausted from a ten to twelve- hour workday and have to deal with someone else's belongings.

At the end of long and often intense days at work, I still had several big jobs to complete before I could take care of myself.

No matter how late the hour, I had to fix dinner, care for EJ, take care of his meds, bathe him, and get him to bed. If I was lucky, he cooperated with each step. Frequently, he didn't. I hoped that he'd sleep through the night, but I couldn't count on it. The result was that I often got no more than a few hours of uninterrupted sleep.

So, the knitting bag bothered me. It took up space, was in my way and, to me, was unsightly.

Just looking at it made me feel much the same as having sand in my shoe. No matter how small an issue, it was an irritant I couldn't ignore for long. I invested way too much time trying to assign meaning to her decision to leave the bag in such an obvious place. Yet, I couldn't figure it out. I didn't think Cheryl was upset at staying late. After all, she'd told me she was happy to get the extra hours and pay.

My thinking was messed up, but I kept going over and over my list of complaints, totally ignoring the true facts of Cheryl's character and, truthfully, my own as well.

At the moment, it felt more rewarding to grouse about her actions than to think reasonably. The best explanation I could come up with was that Cheryl was trying to take over my turf.

Yep! That's it. She's letting me know she's going to do whatever she wants, as if this is her home! And time's up with her "I'm the day-wife" comments. They're not cute or funny. EJ has one wife: there's one Queen of the Castle here, and it's not Cheryl!

Eventually, I grew tired of my internal dialogue, and I decided to act.

I hoisted up the heavy, messy bag and, with a big "Humph," put it in a closet and banged the door shut. Next, I headed straight to the kitchen, and I flipped the glasses back to the "right" way, which just happened to be *my* way. Then I removed Ajax's litter box from the back porch and returned it to its place in the laundry room.

Well, that ought to make things pretty clear! Having reclaimed my turf, I already felt much better.

I said nothing about the bag or other changes when I saw Cheryl in the morning. However, she must have discovered them, because the bag was again placed next to the sofa that night. Also, the litter box was on the porch, and the glasses flipped upside down, again.

Game on.

That night, I was especially fed up with not having control of my life, and now, that big, old knitting bag reminded me that I didn't even have control inside of my own home. My angry, tired, put-upon brain decoded Cheryl's actions as passive-aggressive.

I decided to reclaim my home, for good.

For sure, this was not my finest hour; but I was not myself. In retrospect, I was petty and unkind as I plotted my counterattack. Worse yet, I enjoyed my scheming.

This time, I put the knitting bag in a different closet. I also flipped each glass to rest with the rim up. I put a note on the cat box, "Ajax can't find his box at night. Please leave it here or I will leave his 'stuff' for you to clean up in the morning." I went to bed with a sense of triumph.

It didn't last long.

The morning rush to get ready for work prohibited me from reversing my stupid choices of the night before. Throughout the day, I thought about my actions with aching regret. I considered calling her but decided it was best to apologize to Cheryl in person for my prior night's temper tantrum.

In my mind, I played out a variety of excuses to give her for my actions. They were all flimsy and pathetic. And they were lies . . . I was not, in fact, under the influence of some mistakenly taken drug, aliens had not numbed my brain for twelve hours and, no, Ajax, despite his many talents, had not written the note.

After weighing my options, I decided to tell the simple truth and prayed it wouldn't ruin our relationship. In fact, I greatly valued Cheryl's friendship, trustworthiness, and devotion to my husband's care, and I wanted her to know it.

However, when I got home that night, Cheryl rushed past me and waved goodbye without speaking. We didn't even make eye contact. My heart sank.

I did a quick check around the house and discovered that the bag was gone. The glasses were left as I had arranged them. The cat's litter box was in its usual place, but my note had been removed.

Cheryl's three-word note was left for me in the normal spot on the kitchen counter.

"I get it."

Through my fatigue, imaginings, and frustration, I had engaged in behavior that jeopardized a very meaningful relationship and risked losing the support of an outstanding partner in my husband's care. Cheryl's friendship meant so much to me, but I almost threw it all away over a knitting bag.

Thankfully, Cheryl had risen above my pettiness.

A truce had been declared and peace restored, for both of us. Our relationship continued for years with no further conflicts, while our mutual affection and respect deepened. I learned much later that, after EJ became a permanent resident in a long-term care facility, Cheryl had continued her weekly visits with him. She did this out of pure affection for him, without pay or acknowledgment.

How blessed we were that she chose to be a part of our family!

When you need help, it's not always easy to let someone into your home. However, the benefits of finding the right partner-in-care are tremendous. I am so grateful for the caring support, both for my husband and myself, from so many extraordinary people. We've been truly blessed to have them in our lives.

My hope is that if the need arises, you too will find a perfect match and a true partner-in-care.

STEPPINGSTONES

- ∾ Understand when we need help and adjust to these changing circumstances.

- ∾ Carefully select our partners-in-care, deal with them honestly and respectfully, and express gratitude for their service.

- ∾ Pick my battles, resolve the issues, and move on.

- ∾ Nothing nor anyone can threaten my relationship with my husband; that's the deal we made with each other. Don't let my fears convince me otherwise.

CHAPTER 10

The Winding Road to Recovery

*This is my direction to you, be strong
and courageous; don't be afraid nor discouraged:
for I am the Lord your God, and I am with you
throughout it all, no matter what comes your way.
You are my beloved daughter.*
Joshua 1:9

*She rises while it is yet night, to care
for her family. She is wise and uses her resources
carefully. She has a strong spirit and is grateful
for the work that provides for her loved ones
and they reap the rewards of her efforts. She is
blessed and the Lord provides
a bounty of riches to her.*
Proverbs 31:15-17

*I discovered that my burdens were really blessings
and challenges necessary for my growth.*
- James Christensen

A caregiver will do anything to help the one in their charge.
They will try any new idea.

I did.

Stay up all night doing research.

I did.

Desperately seek the advice of anyone who will give it—without thinking through the consequences—only to have it turn out to be a costly mistake.

I did.

At great expense, engage a transcendental meditation guru to help calm your loved one's mind, only to later realize your loved one has no memory of the needed practices and discipline. Hire a personal in-home fitness trainer and discover that most of their time is spent swapping stories about the good old days. Learn that neither a guru nor a fitness trainer offers money-back guarantees.

I did.

Buy any and every kind of exercise equipment that looks promising. Spend thousands of dollars you can't afford in search of the Holy Grail that will aid in your loved one's recovery. Discover that the items weren't a match, adaptable to his condition or helpful with his ever-changing needs. Sometimes my best intentions actually jeopardized my husband's safety.

Rather than housing the biggest private collection of exercise equipment, sell everything at a great financial loss or give them away for free.

I did.

Join a support group sponsored by a hospital or other reputable organization.

I did.

While I know these groups can be very helpful for others, this was not an answer for my husband or me. Following the recommendation of his doctor, we attended the Stroke Support Group meeting, sponsored by the hospital. After just one meeting, I decided we wouldn't attend again. It was a struggle to work one more appointment into our schedules, and the benefits were marginal. Also, my husband didn't have the experience I'd anticipated.

His response to the evening shattered my heart.

On the way home, EJ shared that he didn't know why he was at the hospital again. He was upset and confused by all "the very sick people" and declared he wasn't as bad off as they were. His primary fear was we were really there to admit him to the hospital again.

"Please don't leave me there again, please don't do it! I'll get better, I promise." EJ repeatedly said, no matter how many times I reassured him. I gave my husband my word we would not return to the meetings unless he asked to attend one.

This continued all the way home. Once home, I was able to better comfort him and settle him into bed. I stayed by his side until he eventually fell asleep.

I, on the other hand, stayed awake for hours thinking about other ways to find help for us and prayed for guidance.

Still, despite our experience, I'd encourage anyone to give a support group a try. However, I strongly recommend that you pay close attention to how *both* of you are feeling about the experience.

Hopefully, you and yours will find the comfort, resources and support you are seeking.

Tools, Tips and Hacks

Caregivers spend a lot of time pursuing solutions to their loved one's current set of challenges. Everyone's needs are different, and they are subject to ongoing change. There is no one magic answer or prescription that fits someone's ever-changing needs.

In our case, speech, strength, and mobility were the main targets of the recovery efforts. The doctors and therapists addressed the loss of the full right side of his brain as best as they could. However, it was my job to try to figure out how best to make things work for us at home and throughout our routine activities. As EJ's conditions and needs kept changing, I did my best to keep up with the very fluid situation.

It was a big job!

Thankfully, today the resources available to provide for a variety of needs continue to expand greatly. There are now remote caregiving apps, fall detection devices and emergency alert systems. In addition to your normal online research, be sure to check out the recommendations from organizations such as AARP, specific support groups and other community resources. And of course, never be too shy to ask others if they have any ideas that might help with your situation.

However, many of these resources weren't available during our time of need.

Here are some tools I found to be helpful and well worth the investment when dealing with a variety of physical challenges. Many are just common sense, but they weren't common to me. I had to figure things out along the way. Hopefully, other caregivers are far more knowledgeable coming into their roles than I was, but even if that's the case, it's good to be reminded of these simple aids and easily achievable actions. While benefit coverages vary and you may have a copay, the marked items (*) are generally covered through an insurance company. Before purchasing anything, check with your plan to see if a doctor's prescription is required for the items to be covered.

Best advice ever: do your homework before you buy something. Don't spend your precious financial resources (a.k.a money) before knowing the details of the full benefits coverage available for your loved one!

Amazon is a great place to start your research and you'll be able to easily compare pricing on items. A basic search of "disability aids" or "physical therapy aids" will bring up many products that you may find useful.

Critical Information

☐ Medical alert bracelets, pendants, home systems, etc. are available in a variety of forms and will provide the basic information needed at a critical time.

☐ ID tags with personal and emergency contact information

☐ Update emergency contact information that may be carried in a wallet or stored in an electronic device.

☐ Provide in-home caregivers with hard copies of your contact information, a backup emergency contact, a prescription list and other information needed by first responders and doctors in case of a medical emergency.

Mobility

☐ Wheelchair, with adjustable footrests*
☐ An extra lightweight wheeled walker or wheelchair for the car*

It may be a luxury to have an extra walker or wheelchair; however, if you can afford it, I highly recommend keeping a lighter version of one of them in the car. They are designed for easier lifting and transport and are especially helpful for short trips and errands—a real help for caregivers on the run!

I suppose it's a personal preference thing, but I didn't like the most commonly used walker. I'm referring to the one that glides rather than rolls. Often, people place split tennis balls on the feet of the walker's legs. We tried using this style of walker, but even after adjusting to the appropriate height, EJ had to constantly stoop over to use it. The walker wasn't easy to manage with one hand, and the tennis ball feet quickly wore out from contact with the sidewalk and parking lot pavement.

The wheeled walker was a far better solution for us and was incredibly helpful when navigating parking lots for doctor visits, etc. The walker should have a bench seat, storage basket and handbrakes. There may be times when a rest is needed, and the bench seat also allows it to be used as a wheelchair when traveling very short distances. If you want this option, be sure to first check with the manufacturer's recommendations.

During a routine visit to our local, big, chain drugstore, I was fortunate enough to spot a brightly colored, aluminum-frame walker for sale. It looked like a jazzy bike and had all the bells and whistles I was hoping for, including a bench seat, a cup holder, handbrakes, and a handy storage basket. As an added bonus, it was inexpensive and fit easily within my budget. This walker didn't completely replace the wheelchair but was an invaluable and helpful aid for years. EJ didn't have to stoop over to use it, and he was happy that it gave him the option of having his ever-present water bottle close at hand. When going for walks around the neighborhood, I'd load the basket up with his favorite snacks. We could stop anytime along the way to take a break if he needed one. However, it was more often the case that we stopped just because he enjoyed sitting on the bench seat of the walker, munching his snacks, and enjoying the sunshine.

He was one happy dude on these outings, and of course, that made me very happy.

❐ Quad cane*

There are differing opinions about quad canes. We preferred it because it could stand on its own when use of the hand was needed for something else and seemed to provide more stability than a regular cane.

If you choose to use one, be sure to adjust the height to fit the user's needs. Also, be aware that the two sides of the base may have different widths. Many can be swiveled to accommodate the user's dominant hand, that is whether they are a lefty or right-handed. Be sure that the cane is adjusted accordingly, or the user may end up tripping themselves because the too-wide base is projecting into their foot path.

☐ Shopping Carts

Electric shopping carts, available in many stores, didn't work well for us. My husband was confused about the controls and, if he did manage to operate it, did so with no regard for the other shoppers. He was unsafe at any speed. It was a far better solution to have him push the regular cart with me in the lead. We made slow progress down the aisles, but he gained at least some small feeling of independence and exercise.

Still, even something as seemingly simple as the use of a shopping cart is a highly individualized decision. As always, you'll figure out what's best for your own circumstances.

Clothing

Many wonderful options can be found through an "adaptive clothing" online search. However, you may also be able to simplify the dressing process through better choices with routine clothing items. The following worked well for us, and I didn't need to spend money on specialty clothing items.

☐ Socks with non-skid soles, great for wearing to bed in case there needs to be a trip to the bathroom during the night.

- ☐ Pull-up pants and shorts with elastic waist bands or tie up options.

- ☐ Tops/shirts that open on the front.

- ☐ Shoes and other apparel items with Velcro closures whenever available.

- ☐ Button extenders were new to me. It's a button with an attached elastic loop. The elastic slips around the existing button and the extender button slips through the buttonhole. This provides extra "wiggle room," and the garment becomes much easier to button up.

- ☐ Button hooks are devices that aid someone with limited strength or motion to button and unbutton garments.

- ☐ Another option, if you're handy with a needle and thread, is to replace buttons with large, flat hooks and eyes that are more easily fastened.

- ☐ "No-tie" shoestrings may be new to you. They come in a variety of styles, colors, options, and many different features. The curly, cork-screw ones worked best for us.

- ☐ If no-tie shoestrings are difficult for you to locate or too expensive, you can substitute regular narrow elastic for shoestrings. All you need is elastic and a pair of scissors; no sewing is required! If you're going to use this homemade version, after lacing the shoe, tie the bow with a double knot. *Hooray!* You have converted lace-up shoes into slip-ons.

- ☐ Slip-on shoes/slippers are also great choices, and a large variety of inexpensive options are available.

NOTE: Mark all clothing items with the loved one's name. You never know when another hospital or other facility stay may be necessary. It's so comforting to be prepared for these unplanned circumstances. Additionally, any items that will be used while your loved one is residing and receiving care outside of the home should be inexpensive and easily replaced, should they become lost or stolen.

Experience says you'll encounter both of these situations.

Bathing/Shower Aids

☐ Water socks/shoes for the shower or bathtub

What a difference this non-slip footwear makes!

The potential danger of slips and falls in wet areas will become greatly reduced if, before bathing or showering, the person wears "reef runner" type shoes. These are very inexpensive and available in most discount stores. The prices vary, but even the least expensive pairs last a long time. After bathing, the wearer will have enough traction to rise out of the tub, and they will also be much more secure when they are on wet shower floors.

☐ Shower chair/bench*

☐ Showerhead/handheld combo

These are always wonderful, but especially useful for someone with limited mobility or standing issues. If budget is an issue, look for options you will be able to easily install yourself. I promise, the first one I bought attached as easily as a garden hose to the outside faucet. Tip: if available, take the time to read the installation instructions before purchasing the item. If it's too complicated, keep searching for other options that are easier to install!

- ☐ Slip-resistant mats for the shower or bathtub
- ☐ Long-handled body scrubber*
- ☐ Easily accessible shelf/bench for hair/body care products
- ☐ All product containers should have pump dispensers or squeeze tops. These are more manageable for those individuals with limited hand strength or usage.

If bar soap is preferred, consider placing it inside of a clean sock, tied off or secured closed with a rubber band. This makes the soap far easier to handle, and the sock doubles as a washcloth. When it's time to launder the sock, remove the soap and simply treat it as you would any other washcloth.

- ☐ Hooks/racks installed for easier access to washcloths and towels
- ☐ Fog-free large shower mirror, located at eye level when seated on shower chair/bench
- ☐ Lightweight bath towels are the easiest to manage with limited strength or only one functioning hand. I switched out our luxurious large towels and washcloths for waffle-textured ones. I purchased them from Ikea. They were inexpensive, easy to handle and dried quickly, a perfect choice for us!

General Independence, Self-Care

- ☐ Raised commode seat with side grab bars*
- ☐ Extended length reacher. * Looks like a giant pincer for reaching for items on the floor or just out of reach
- ☐ Gripper mats/pads to open items. Use multiple ones to place under the item and on top.
- ☐ Long handled shoehorn*
- ☐ Sock assist aid*
- ☐ Large head toothbrush
- ☐ Electric shaver
- ☐ Wall grab bars in commode and shower areas*

Eating

- ☐ "Rocker knife"
- ☐ Adaptive utensils with wide, non-slip handles
- ☐ Other specialty tableware and drinkware; weighted or melamine worked best for us.
- ☐ Dealing with perception issues. After some time, I noticed EJ's pattern of only eating items on the right side of his plate, yet he claimed to still be hungry. I was concerned and spoke to the doctor about this new behavior. He explained to me that this was a matter of perception, not an issue with EJ's vision. He offered a simple solution: to slowly rotate the plates as EJ finished one section. It worked like a charm!

☐ Bibs and other protective items. I first became aware of adult bibs while observing an elderly woman in a restaurant with her husband who appeared to have several physical limitations. Before dining, she lovingly placed an oversized, probably homemade, bib around his neck. It was a practical solution for both of them. If the need for this article arises, here's the good news: you don't need to be a seamstress. There are now many options for you to choose from online.

Medications

☐ Pill organizer tray with lid
☐ Pill cutter

These and so many other wonderful, inexpensive aids are available. You'll find them by doing a simple internet search for "tools to help disabled patients."

Adapting Your Home, Things You Can Do on Your Own

- ☐ Remove rugs or replace with ones that have non-slip backing.

- ☐ Move furniture just enough to create wider access paths.

- ☐ Provide an end table and lighting within reach of the cared one's dominant hand

- ☐ Keeping things simple and having a routine is your friend. Try to keep items, activities, and schedules as uncomplicated as possible.

- ☐ It's very helpful to have bedtimes, personal care activities, and meals follow a scheduled time. Some degree of independence is more easily achieved if routinely used items such as a toothbrush, hairbrush, etc. are returned to the same location after each use.

- ☐ A magnetic whiteboard and marker are great ways to communicate, especially when another caregiver is on duty.

One day, a neighbor shared that my husband had developed a new afternoon routine that neither Cheryl nor I were aware was happening. Evidently, while he was supposed to be taking a nap, he was slipping out the back door and stopping at various neighbors' homes where he asked to join them for a beer and a chat. If the neighbor had time for a visit, they sat together on the front porch. If not, he would "go visiting," as he put it, at the next house. When EJ finished his rounds, he'd slip back into the bedroom without being noticed.

Our neighbor made it very clear to me that, although EJ was always welcomed, he and others in the neighborhood were concerned that we may not be aware of his afternoon social life routine.

Indeed, we were not!

Almost immediately, I installed message boards on the inside of every exterior door with messages about staying home, checking with the caregiver for a treat or beverage, etc. It worked; he followed the written directions and didn't go visiting and asking for beer from the neighbors again.

That I know of.

On the main door's message board, I wrote a "Good Morning" message and listed the day of the week and date. I also included my expected time home.

My sweetest days were when I found a new, shakily written "I love you too" message on the board.

☐ Cellphone, tablet, earbuds, and stand: having these available may be a luxury, but if you can afford them, they are so helpful for all of you.

It's a way to stay in touch with distant family and friends as well as provide entertainment and games that can be helpful therapy.

However, assess your situation very carefully! I learned the hard way that I had not taken the proper precautions to ensure my husband's cognitive issues didn't make him vulnerable to online scams and ridiculous purchases. Delete any apps that involve purchases or sharing of personal information.

Maybe you'll be able to avoid receiving a case of Tigers Blood Miracle Memory pills, as happened at our home.

☐ This is more for the caregiver than for the one they're responsible for: consider hiding the remote! If the person is experiencing confusion, the TV remotes will only frustrate them. They are likely to hit a series of buttons and make changes to the set-up that will take you forever to detect, understand and correct.

Balance and Falling

EJ's issues with balance and falling were a constant worry for me. No matter his progress in other areas, he remained highly vulnerable to falling. As a result, the threat of his being hurt was ever-present. Unfortunately, I also learned quickly that someone losing their balance can be much like a drowning person who grabs out wildly, further endangering themselves and the rescuer. On more than one occasion, I barely managed not to fall myself, as I tried to steady my husband. There were also times when I was hurt and incurred bruising from these episodes.

It's not easy to prepare for these events, but unfortunately, the person you are caring for may experience them more frequently with time. That was the case for my husband, particularly as his Parkinson's progressed.

During a visit to a large restaurant, I witnessed a mother and daughter attempt to help the father up from his chair. I cringed at what I saw from across the room.

Standing in front and on either side of him, both women grabbed a forearm and tried to pull him up. With each unsuccessful attempt, the poor guy flopped helplessly back down into his seat. The women were almost knocked to the floor in the process. I gasped and stood to help, but before I could reach them, somehow, after several more attempts, they managed to get him standing and connected with his walker. All three looked frazzled from the event.

How I wish they'd had the benefit of a good therapist showing them the right way to assist a disabled person while minimizing the possibility of stress and harm to the one in their care and themselves!

My advice is to think ahead about potential causes of falls and how you will navigate obstacles, be observant of your surroundings and adjust accordingly. You'll need to experiment to find what works best for the two of you in a variety of situations.

For instance, when walking short distances without the walker or stepping off a curb, I found we were both more secure and steady on our feet when EJ used my shoulder as a brace, rather than my arm.

Going up or coming down the stairs presented equal challenges. In addition to areas in the bathroom, I had handrails professionally installed on both sides of the staircases. This proved to be a huge benefit for both of us. Whether it was the fear of slipping or actual loss of balance, at least one of us was able to safely grab a handrail at all times.

Of course, once someone *has* fallen, your first step is to ascertain if they are injured and if calling 911 for emergency assistance is required. This did occur several times for us. However, it was more often the case of a loss of footing with no injuries. In each case, at any hour, the caregiver has to determine the next best course of action.

Although the fall may not be serious, the caregiver must still exercise caution when assisting the other person. The fallen person may not have control of their limbs, not be able to help themselves or be experiencing a sort of "dead weight" (a term I hate) which makes it much more difficult to help them and possibly dangerous for the caregiver. Also, helping the person back up may be a challenge because of size differences and the strength required to assist them.

I'd learned from the therapists that it's very helpful to move a chair close to the fallen person. It's far easier to move them halfway up, rather than attempt a full stand. Let the one you've assisted rest in the chair a few minutes before attempting to move them to a standing position.

Sometimes the best way to help someone back up from the floor is to exercise a little patience. In my experience, trying to get my husband immediately back on his feet wasn't always the best solution for him or me.

I learned the value of patience in these situations the hard way.

In preparation for the next day's busy schedule at the VA, I had just gotten us settled into bed a little earlier than normal. We both fell quickly asleep. All was well, until I heard EJ call my name in the middle of the night.

He had fallen while returning from the restroom and was on the floor near the foot of the bed. He wasn't hurt, but because of his balance issues, try as I might, I couldn't assist him to get back on his feet. For me, it was like trying to lift a 178-pound wet noodle. After several attempts, we were both exhausted from our efforts. Eventually, I decided to pull the comforter and pillows off the bed and made a pallet for us on the floor. It was very uncomfortable, but it was a good trade in exchange for some more sleep.

I awoke in the early morning to find myself alone on the floor without covers. EJ, on the other hand, was nestled snugly in the bed with the comforter pulled up to his chin. Evidently, sometime during the night, he had managed to stand up on his own and reclaim both the bed and the covers.

At least one of us was well-rested for the day ahead; one of us was quite cranky from sleeping on the floor.

Perhaps, if I'd waited a little longer between the attempts to get him into a chair or onto his feet, we might have both enjoyed a good night's rest.

Perhaps, perhaps, perhaps...

Sleep Issues

As my husband experienced the onset and progression of Parkinson's disease, he began to have tremors throughout the night. These increased as the condition advanced. While he usually slept through them, I was continually awakened by his strong, jerky movements.

Eventually, the lack of sleep really impacted my ability to accomplish my responsibilities the following day. Increasingly, I was experiencing a lack of energy and varying levels of "brain fog."

Others have told me they opted for separate beds as their loved one's physical conditions worsened. I couldn't do it; I wanted my husband near me, no matter what his condition. Not only was this an emotional decision, but I also believed it increased my chances of being aware of any issues he might experience during the night. It didn't always work, but for the most part, I was right.

Fortunately, as we shared a coffee break, a colleague told me of something that helped him under similar circumstances. I took his advice. Although it was costly, buying a new memory foam mattress was the perfect answer for both of us. EJ was able to adjust his position more easily, and I was no longer impacted by his tremors. We both were able to rest better throughout the whole night.

In spite of his limited mobility, it wasn't unusual for EJ to get up on his own during the night. At times he'd wander through the house, confused about his surroundings or the time of night. Of course, this concerned me for many reasons. Usually, I was able to quickly find him and safely bring him back to bed.

I was never able to completely eliminate these episodes. Eventually however, I remembered my long-ago training for some Girl Scout badge. After he was in bed for the night, I rigged up a sort of bedrail next to his side of the bed. I placed a kitchen chair seat side out, flat against the bed, about where his shoulders rested. I don't know if this discouraged him from getting up, but the incidents of wandering through the night decreased dramatically. On other nights, when he needed to use the restroom, he began waking me up to help him get out of bed. The simple kitchen chair trick really helped in keeping him safer and therefore, I experienced less worry.

Minimizing Confusion

None of us likes to feel a lack of basic control of our lives. As it related to taking care of our family's needs, this was something of a daily struggle for me. However, my husband's challenges were much more than I could have personally endured. Formerly strongly independent and capable of achieving anything he set his mind on, EJ now grappled to understand elementary concepts, control his emotions and communicate with others. Physically, he had little to no control of his body.

These circumstances often caused him to be depressed, frustrated and angry. At other times, he apologized for his condition and vowed to get better, for me. I'm not sure which episode was more heartbreaking to witness.

While I was forced to acknowledge some things wouldn't change (*at least not yet*, the optimist in me asserted), I realized I was capable of taking control of other areas that improved EJ's experience.

My goal was to create a familiar environment that helped my husband feel more connected and independent. Although maintaining a routine was very difficult, several small changes in our daily activities proved to be immensely helpful.

The advice I received from medical professionals was invaluable and is worth sharing with others. To the extent that you are able, try to keep bedtimes, mealtimes, walks, chores, and relaxing activities as consistent as possible. Keep items, especially personal articles, in the same location. Be mindful to place these items within reach of the person's dominant hand and return them to the same place after each use or cleaning.

When in the company of others, use the other people's names frequently. This is a handy prompt for your loved one and may also help them avoid embarrassment and frustration with themselves.

Other than creating wider pathways around the home, avoid making big changes in furniture arrangement or redecoration. Even something as simple as keeping their preferred snacks in the same place can make their life easier.

At last, we had a workable routine. I thought I'd figured it all out and things would be okay from now on. I anticipated EJ's recovery would continue on pace, and we'd soon have our nice little life back.

How could I have known what lay ahead?

STEPPINGSTONES

∞ Healing is often invisible; recovery isn't always linear. I can't be discouraged just because I don't see progress at the moment.

∞ Little changes can make big differences. I can do a lot to make things better for both of us.

∞ Trial and error are not failures. They are building blocks to a better way, a better solution. Be kind to myself when they feel like stumbling blocks. "Suck it up, Buttercup," get back on my feet and try again.

∞ I'm not superhuman. Sometimes, I need to get help and advice to figure this all out.

CHAPTER 11

In-Patient Rehabilitation and Long-Term Care Facilities

*I can count on this; we are safe. The Lord will pre-
serve us from all evil: he will preserve our souls.
The Lord shall preserve our going out
and our coming in from this time forward,
and even for evermore.*
Psalm 121: 7-8

*Grant me the serenity to accept the things
I cannot change, the courage to change the things
I can, and the wisdom to know the difference.*
- Reinhold Niebuhr

EJ's recovery—no, it's more honest to say his life—was a constant roller coaster of small , hopeful signs of progress to devastating reversals of physical health as well as mental and emotional well-being.

We were in a constant state of flux.

As my husband's medical needs changed throughout the years, he experienced multiple hospitalizations and stays in skilled nursing and rehabilitation facilities. Once home again, the type and level of home care also fluctuated to meet his ever-changing medical status.

All these facilities and services are in high demand. The physician, insurance plan and, if applicable, the Department of Veteran Affairs (VA) have a great deal to do with the type of care the patient receives and the designated facility. Based upon demand, services offered and proximity to your home, you may have to make some difficult decisions and tradeoffs to ultimately secure the best spot and care available for your loved one.

The following may be helpful as you work through the process.

Facility Selection Criteria, in no particular order:

- ❑ Check out state ratings and understand the rating criteria.
- ❑ Tour the facility.

Do a careful review of the cafeteria, posted menus, general cleanliness, and postings on bulletin boards. Postings should include state-required ratings/data etc. In the cafeteria, check out the weekly menu. If there isn't one, ask "Why not?"

Whenever I could manage it, without going through closed doors or being too obvious, I wandered through "Employee Only" areas. You can learn about the company's culture and how the administration treats their staff by taking this extra step. Look for postings that include employee recognition announcements, customer service letters of gratitude, and other positive and motivating messages. Are there photos of the team or community activities? Or are there bold, warning messages signed by an authoritarian entity known universally as "The Management"? You don't have the right to ask to see these areas, but if you manage to get a peek, are their break areas clean and at least reasonably furnished?

Why does all this matter? It matters because the company's true behind-the-scenes culture reflects how the employees will treat your loved one.

☐ Is there an unpleasant smell of body odor, urine or other indicators of poor patient care and the facility's general cleanliness?

☐ Overall, visible cleanliness of the facility: trust your gut. For instance, sticky floors are a major clue that improvement is needed in other areas, as well.

☐ Consider proximity to the nearest health-care facility.

☐ How close is it to your home? How far will you need to travel to visit?

☐ Is the facility secure? How is that security maintained?

☐ Is it light and bright? Do the rooms have windows?

☐ Are there outside areas available to the residents to enjoy the fresh air and sunshine?

☐ What is the family's involvement in Care Plan Meetings?

☐ What rehabilitation therapy is available? What is the therapy schedule for your loved one's condition?

☐ Are there social activities and other group interactions for the residents?

- [ ] Are there large communal spaces for watching TV, visiting with other residents, playing piano, etc.?

- [ ] What spiritual support resources are available? Is there a designated chaplain, visiting clergy schedule, a space designated as a chapel, and are religious services conducted on the premises?

- [ ] How do the rooms of current patients appear? Are they overcrowded? Are patients "parked" in hallways during the day? If so, regardless of their physical state, do the patients appear alert or drugged and disconnected from their environment?

- [ ] How often are patients seen by doctors?

- [ ] What nursing staff is on duty 24/7?

- [ ] What services are provided, i.e., laundry, nail care, hair, transportation to medical appointments, etc.?

- [ ] Understand whether these services are included in the fees or if you are personally responsible for them.

- [ ] Understand all fees, applicable insurance benefits and anything else you will be responsible for financially.

- [ ] Inspect the designated room with the same level of detail you would if you were purchasing a new home. In a sense, you are. Is the room's space acceptable and has natural light? Are all items in working order? Is the furniture in good repair and functioning properly? Be sure to check the nurse's call button, TV remote, air conditioning, the phone, and the controls on the bed. Multiple times, I've had to request repairs and replacements of items. These included changing out inoperable call buttons, dresser drawers, broken chairs, and dead batteries in remotes.

☐ These things may also be indicators concerning the quality of the management of other areas, including care, food, facility maintenance and administrative standards.

☐ What are the guidelines regarding visitors?

☐ Observe interactions between staff and existing patients. Do they exchange greetings, make eye contact, etc.? Does the staff refer to patients by their names?

☐ What is the general environment like? If the need arose, would you want to stay there?

Life on the Inside

My role as a caregiver didn't stop once my husband was admitted to a long-term care facility. The responsibilities of ensuring his safety and care, as well as handling all financial and domestic matters, were still mine. The only things that changed were how I executed them.

If you face a similar situation, the sooner you truly realize the person you care for is now living in a communal environment, the better. In other words, while from a broad perspective you still maintain responsibility for your loved one's care, you will have little control over their day-to-day experience. Yet, there are some things you can do to make this a more comfortable and safe experience for them. You may also be able to reduce the likelihood of theft or "misplacement" of their personal belongings.

Think about it. What would you do if you were sending a child off to camp? You would boldly mark all personal belongings with the person's name and, depending upon the anticipated length of stay, include their room number. This includes all clothing, shoes (we had shoes stolen at least ten times), undergarments, socks, and anything else you wish to remain yours.

It works well to have a general schedule for your visits. Your loved one will appreciate a schedule, feel less abandoned in between visits, and find comfort in knowing that you will soon be there. However, to get a 360-view of the staff and conditions at the facility, also make additional random visits at different times of day or night.

Know the staff and remember their names. Also, this should go without saying but is easy to overlook, treat all levels of staff, from the cleaning person to the doctor, with equal respect. Your loved one is in the care of them all, 24/7. They deserve your appreciation.

Notice any bruising, scabs, infections, odd odors, etc. Ask the charge nurse to look at them with you and discuss the possible causes and remedies.

Here are some ideas on how to maximize your loved one's comfort and care while in a facility away from home.

Personal Care:

- Dry spray shampoo is a tremendous help to freshen up the patient's hair between showers.

- Disposable bath/body wipes are also another great way to quickly freshen up the one you care for.

- For men, bring an electric razor on your visits. It gives the patient a safe way to groom themselves and no one can steal the razor when you're not there. We "lost" a few before I began taking it home with me after each visit.

- Even though barber services could be purchased, I elected to cut his hair. It was simple to keep up with and made him feel so much better.

- Initially, I wasn't aware that nail care is generally not included as a routine service. I wrongly assumed his toenails were being looked after. As a result of this misunderstanding, a problem developed. It was eventually corrected but could have easily been avoided had I understood my responsibilities more clearly.

Laundry:

- I strongly recommend that you do your own laundry if it's logistically feasible for you. While having laundry provided is a nice perk, it's very common for your items to go missing, even if they are clearly labeled with your loved one's name.

- I also preferred using laundry products I trusted and with scents familiar to my husband. Later, when his confusion had him believe that he was on vacation rather than a long-term care facility, EJ often commented that "this hotel smells like home." Most certainly, he could only have been referring to the scent of his fresh laundry from home.

Shared Spaces:

- If the room is semi-private, introduce yourself to the other person. Interact with them, but don't assume they want to be part of your ongoing conversations.

- Honor the roommate's privacy and give them space when they have visitors.

- If sharing a room with another patient, draw the bed curtain when you wish to create at least the illusion of privacy for your loved one. Consider that it is highly likely that whatever you say will be heard by someone else, including their personal visitors.

- Often, the other person is immobile and will be present in the room most of the time. Even though the drapes may be closed, it's not unusual for the other person to join in the conversation. Most of the time it's harmless banter, but it can still feel a bit intrusive. It helps to remember that their shared space is, for the most part, the total of their lonely, small world. Include them if they want to be a part of your visit, but also gently redirect the conversation if it's stealing too much personal time from you and your loved one.

- There may be times when it's necessary for the two of you to have confidential discussions regarding financial or other family matters. Also, you want to be able to ask questions about any concerns they may have about the treatment they're receiving. Seek privacy, as needed, to ensure your loved one is able to give authentic feedback about their feelings concerning the facility and the treatment they receive from the staff.

Creating Private, Personalized Experiences:

- Take the one you care for outdoors, if possible. If that's not available, simply getting them out of the room, going up and down the corridors or finding a quiet corner does a lot to lift their spirits. I never hesitated to ask for the staff to facilitate our little adventures by getting my husband into a wheelchair.

One of our favorite shared times was to "sneak" into the closed cafeteria. I'd unload his favorite snacks and cold drinks from home and turn up the music on my phone. Usually, he'd ask me to dance with him. We'd join hands; EJ seated in his wheelchair, me standing, facing him. We'd sway to the beat and often sing along with the oldies. You see, we still had the moves; they just didn't look the same.

Nonetheless, we were happy in our little, private corner of the world.

- Bring your loved one outside meals and favorite treats within any restrictions. I admit, I was often tempted to circumvent these rules. But then I'd remember I was working with the healthcare team, not against them . . . well, most of the time.

During one consultation, I asked the doctor if there was any harm in bringing my husband one beer a week. He paused and then answered, "Not really." Those Friday afternoon visits with a bag filled with a hamburger, fries and one or two cold Heinekens were some of the happiest times we shared together.

- Ask if there can be pet visits, but carefully consider the full environment at the facility.

With permission, I took Moondoggy, our eternally youthful-looking dog, on my next visit with EJ. As we walked toward his room, we came upon an elderly woman in a wheelchair parked in the hallway. She sweetly asked if she could hold the dog.

Unaware she suffered from dementia, I happily responded yes.

Immediately she clutched poor Moondoggy so tightly that he began to whimper. The lady then became extremely agitated, started rocking him to and fro, and sternly told him to be quiet. I gently tried to retrieve Moondoggy, but she started crying, calling for help and screaming that I couldn't take *her* dog.

Hearing the commotion, an attendant ran to help us. Fortunately, it ended well for the pup and me, but not so for the poor woman. She was distraught and had to be returned to her room.

My heart ached as they wheeled her away; her cries echoing down the hallway. I felt awful at having caused her so much pain.

Preventing Theft/Lost Articles:

- Keep items of sentimental or monetary value in your personal possession.

- We experienced missing items at every facility, hospitals excluded. Throughout the twenty-two years of what EJ referred to as his "intermittent incarceration," facility administrators told me that they had no control over missing items. They frequently claimed that the items were lost in the laundry (although I did my husband's laundry at home) or blamed the other patients for our losses.

Shoes, in particular, disappeared on a regular basis. No matter how I marked them, nothing, including eventually using bright red nail polish to write EJ's initials on the back of the heels, prevented them from being stolen. No one could claim "they were lost in the laundry" or "your husband left them somewhere," as he wasn't able to put on or remove his shoes by himself. I highly doubted that other patients, with their own set of disabilities, were wrenching the shoes off EJ's feet during the very limited times that he was upright in a wheelchair.

Yet, my reports of the missing shoes were met with no other response than a shrug.

After replacing four pairs of shoes within a few weeks, I gave up and resorted to supplying my husband with cheap slipper socks. No matter how much it bothered me not to be able to keep EJ in shoes, it didn't really matter to him. He was content, and truthfully, that's what I cared about the most. Yet, I still get heartburn just thinking about the lowly worm who would steal from a disabled person; I hate thieves.

- Leave nothing in the facility you will miss if it was stolen or lost. Sadly, this even includes personal jewelry. It's a hard decision to remove something that is precious to both of you, yet I found it necessary. I removed EJ's wedding ring from his hand and opted instead to wear it around my neck on a simple gold chain. That brought me both comfort and sadness by the fact that I needed to take this step to ensure it wasn't stolen from us.

- Before transferring to another facility, take the time to check all personal items.

On one occasion, and for a variety of reasons, my husband was to once again be transferred to a different VA-approved facility.

On the eve of the transfer, I was told the move could occur at any point during the following day. Wanting everything set and ready to go for the morning, I packed his things. Included were many new articles of clothing still bearing their price tags. The next day's transfer was delayed multiple times, and as a result, I was able to finish my workday and be with EJ before the move happened.

As I entered my husband's room, I witnessed an attendant place a large trash bag on the foot of his bed. Before speaking, I glanced around the room, attempting to locate EJ's duffle bag that I had packed the night before. It was nowhere to be seen.

I asked the attendant about the trash bag and was told it contained my husband's belongings that she had personally packed. She very firmly informed me everything was there, and there was no need for me to check her work.

So of course, I did.

In her full view, I pulled rags, most of them women's old worn-out clothing, from the bag. With each item, I called to her, "Not my husband's," and threw the item on the bed. Actually, I threw many of the more absurd items across the room, while continuing to yell. This continued, item by item, until the trash bag was empty.

I was furious and it showed.

Surprisingly, the attendant seemed unfazed, even when I stated that I was ready to resolve the issue with one phone call to the police, but first I wanted to speak with her supervisor. Her calm demeanor led me to believe that she'd run this con game before.

I wasn't aware her boss had already been alerted about the commotion and had just arrived at the door. The attendant fled past her supervisor. I explained what happened and pulled the receipt for the missing items from my purse to back up my claim of over a hundred and fifty dollars of clothing purchases.

As we were speaking, the attendant rolled a large laundry rack into the room, with my husband's empty duffle bag hanging off the top bar. His clothes were all neatly displayed on hangers, their tags still intact.

"Look what I found; these were in the laundry waiting to be washed," she said triumphantly, as if expecting praise for locating the missing items.

Instead, I gave her a disgusted look. The supervisor looked totally bewildered by my reaction and turned to thank the attendant for going the extra mile to locate the items.

I didn't thank her; I knew a thief when I saw one.

After repacking EJ's items, we were on our way to the new facility. I was glad for the change and hoped for a very different set of experiences. I was a bit naïve, and unfortunately, this wouldn't be the last time we experienced theft and dishonesty amongst staff members at my husband's care facilities.

STEPPINGSTONES

- I need to pivot from "the way things used to be" to "the way things can be" and make the most of each new situation.

- Armed with a little creativity, a few precautionary actions, and a lot of love, I will be able to maximize my loved one's experience and my peace of mind.

- The simple things bring so much joy to us both! Treasure the blessings of these times together.

- Stay alert and take action when needed to correct a wrong or neglectful act.

- Control my temper, even if my anger feels justified in the moment. In the long-term, it's better for my well-being, and I don't have to live with the regret of my failing. The scene I created wasn't really necessary or helpful. I need to look for better ways to get the results I seek and have the presence of mind to do it in real-time.

- *Charity also involves patience and is kind; there is no envy or arrogance in those with a charitable heart. Those seeking the perfect way, do not behave in an unbecoming manner, are not easily provoked, and do not think angry, evil thoughts towards others.* 1 Corinthians 13:4-5

I'm still working on this, with varying levels of success.

CHAPTER 12

Communications with Others

When people talk, listen completely.
Most people never listen.
- Ernest Hemingway

The single biggest problem with communication
is the illusion that it has taken place.
- George Bernard Shaw

Avoidance of tough issues, whether through la-
ziness or a lack of confidence lead to defeat and
poverty. However difficult the path may seem;
I will be diligent and will be rewarded accordingly.
Proverbs 10:4

I never anticipated the volume of information I was given and expected to know as I assumed my new caregiver responsibilities. Additionally, I hadn't realized how the exchange of precise details and time-critical communications became an essential part of my life.

With no ramp-up time, I needed to rapidly learn how to manage the excessive two-way and, often, three-way flow of information.

At first, I found it very difficult to process everything, as well as correctly provide the necessary personal health, benefit coverage and financial details to the many others who were reliant upon receiving correct information. Learning to record, track and retrieve significant information was also a challenge for me.

Eventually, I learned to employ messaging strategies that aided in maintaining clear and concise communications in a large variety of circumstances.

You can learn how to enhance your current communication skill set too.

Why bother? It's no bother if it ensures proper care for your loved one and receipt of all available benefits, healthcare coverage and compensation. I discovered that no matter my present skill level of communicating with others, there was always room for improvement and a greater opportunity to achieve the desired results!

The Power of Listening

I confess, the skill of active listening did not come naturally to me. In truth, I was awful at it and still have great room for improvement in this area.

Sad to say, but I preferred being the speaker, the teacher, or the boss rather than having to listen carefully to understand what was needed of me. As one of seven children, there was always competition for attention and getting my share of "air space" in the conversation at the dinner table. I suppose this may have contributed to my lack of listening expertise. Or maybe it's just my nature to attempt to dominate a conversation; I'm not sure and it doesn't really matter. However, as a result of my habits, I often missed important information and nuances that certainly would have made my life easier had I truly heard them the first time. The leadership training courses I attended on this topic were interesting, but the effects were short-term only.

It's so hard to break old habits.

The pre-stroke me hadn't seriously thought of the power of listening as a way to make better decisions and, frankly, be a better person for others. Yet suddenly, I was involved in conversations that had serious consequences if I made the wrong decisions. In many situations, the post-stroke me lacked the knowledge needed to under-stand the issues or a grasp of the necessary administrative procedures and financial issues where there was no room for error.

After experiencing some major misses, I realized there was very little time to improve my skills in this area. I had to become a better listener, and I had to make the needed progress quickly.

I learned to compartmentalize and shut down dis-tracting thoughts and actually listen to what was being said in the moment.

Rather than interrupt the speaker, I made notes of my follow-up questions. Quite frequently, by letting the speaker finish without interruption, these questions were already addressed before I needed to refer to my notes. And in fact, the information given was usually far more helpful than if the conversation had been limited to the direction I was going to pursue.

Very early in my caregiver experience, I quit worrying about appearing stupid to others. This was especially true when conversing with doctors and other professionals in-volved in EJ's care. Again, I simply had no choice but to make this transition. I asked questions when I didn't understand something, including jargon, abbreviations, medical terms, acronyms, etc. Soon, I forgot about how I might appear to others and just took care of the business before me.

I observed and "listened" to nonverbal cues, whenev-er possible. This was always a helpful tool. My ability to "read the audience" improved with practice. If the other person was short, even terse or rushed, I shifted gears and went straight for the boiled-down version of what we needed to communicate. This method was generally effective, and I received so much help, simply by demonstrating that I respected the other person's time.

However, if it appeared the other person had the time and was willing to share more, I took advantage of their openness and asked for more advice, information, additional resources, etc. Engaging others who were willing to participate in more of a relationship rather than a transactional exchange was always very helpful and satisfying to both of us. For some, they were able to fulfill their need to be of help; others welcomed the opportunity to demonstrate their expertise. There were undoubtedly times when both of these needs were met for the person helping me. Whatever their personal motivations may have been, I was grateful for their guidance.

Summarizing a conversation and asking for verification that I got it right also became routine. Usually, I was on track with the other person. However, sometimes I discovered that I had missed an important point or entirely misunderstood something. These extra steps provided an opportunity for clarification, correction, or expansion on the details, when needed.

Simply put, I became a much better communicator when I broadened my skills tool kit, learned to pause, and more adeptly evaluate the situation before speaking, and adjusted my communication methods accordingly.

Administrative Conversations Regarding Employment, Benefits Coverage and Other Critical Matters

Keeping a log of each conversation with medical professionals, hospital administrators, both of our employers and all benefits representatives proved to be the single most critical step in my communications process.

I think maintaining up-to-date, hard copy records are best for prolonged issues, but that's me.

My preferred method was using a simple legal pad. As I filled one log up, I set it aside and started another one. The filled ones were then stored in an inexpensive canvas storage bin I got from a discount store. Eventually, these bins fully occupied one of my kitchen counters.

You may prefer making notes on an electronic device, in a notebook or common theme book. You will find something that perfectly suits your needs and administrative skills.

Whatever recordkeeping method you select, keep it handy and updated in real-time.

The result will be that you have an accurate, chronological record of these various conversations, covering multiple topics. And most importantly, you'll be able to easily retrieve the information you need, when you need it.

And you will need it.

There are many reasons you will need to repeatedly reference these notes and dates. Staff members change, others have a different recollection than you, you may be challenged on the outcomes of prior conversations, etc.

I experienced all these issues, as well as some flat-out deceptive people. Ah, but I never lost a battle with one of those, and neither will you if you keep proper notes.

Another important tip is whether these communications were on the phone or in person, I always pleasantly let the other person know that I was taking notes and asked for clarification of the correct spelling of their name and title. Additionally, I asked for confirmation of the date and time. Something like this, "Okay, for my notes, today is October fifth at ten thirty-five, right? Is that the time you have?"

The benefits of this small step were enormous. It both improved the quality of our immediate conversation and my long-term recordkeeping. Also, there was a frequent need to follow up on the prior conversations and having the person's name, date and other details of the call made a tremendous difference in establishing my credibility and getting issues resolved.

I also believe that my transparent intent to clarify and record our conversation, as well as the outcome, kept us both focused on the issues and resulted in a more productive dialogue.

Maintaining this log needn't be as daunting as it may sound, especially if you prepare a basic outline in advance of the conversation. Update the main points as the discussion is happening or immediately afterwards.

Don't wait! Complete your notes as soon as the call or visit is over. Things change and move quickly. You can't afford to rely on your memory or having the right time in the future to accurately reconstruct a conversation.

At the top of a fresh page, include the following:

- Day of the week, date, and time
- Contact name and title
- Company affiliation
- Direct line phone number
- Subject of discussion
- As needed, any relevant policy/ID numbers
- Bullet points about the discussion
- Include any questions you asked and the responses given
- Conclude with the agreed-upon next steps
- Trace in your calendar any follow-up dates

The benefits of this log are multifold.

First, there is the obvious value of having some record of the multiple issues and needed actions you are dealing with.

Second, in the midst of all this unplanned chaos, it will bring you peace and order to know that you can go back to your notes for anything you may have missed or need to follow up with others.

Thirdly, when dealing with benefits representatives, it's important to refer with accuracy to important dates, forms requested and submitted, etc. These records were invaluable to me when I needed to provide proof of prior conversations, context of those conversations, pending items and resulting decisions/directions.

We are surrounded by good people who are willing to help us if given the opportunity. In particular, I found medical professionals and administrative staff provided very valuable information in response to the following questions:

- Is there anything else I should know?
- I'm sorry, I don't understand what that means. Can you please explain it a little differently?
- Is there anything else you would recommend?
- What are the next steps?
- What do you advise?
- If EJ was a member of your family, what would you do?

Interactions with
Medical Professionals

Professionally, I was very fortunate to be given employment opportunities that, while they may have required relocation, always aligned with my husband's everchanging medical situation and our financial needs.

Actually, this was much more than good fortune. Whenever we had a need, we were blessed in ways I could not have foreseen.

As a consequence of moving around the country—on average every thirty months—my husband frequently had new doctors and medical support teams. It was of great importance that each doctor saw EJ as much more than the culmination of his disability, illness, or disease. Before discussing the stroke or the other medical issues as they emerged throughout the years, I began each visit with a new physician by presenting my husband as a whole person, not just a set of physical conditions.

My first priority was to explain to the doctors, intentionally within my husband's earshot, that his new patient was an extraordinary person.

"This is a man who matters. He is deeply loved and treasured by our family and friends. Professionally, he is immensely respected by his colleagues both for who he is and for his contributions to the space program. In addition to several other awards and recognition, he has received the prestigious Silver Snoopy Award from the astronauts. EJ is a good man, and he makes a difference in this world to many, many people. We need him. We have faith in you and your contributions to his recovery."

I never received a negative reaction to that introduction. In fact, wherever we were, whatever the circumstances, my husband received excellent care from his primary care physicians.

Although we never spoke of my comments to the doctors, I am sure EJ benefited from the reminder of his precious value to all of us. It was good for my husband to have his worth reaffirmed outside of the family. I hoped that these words also helped to combat his frequent feelings of being a burden to others, but particularly to me. Sadly, these thoughts were crushing for him and hard for me to overcome.

All I could do was to be sure he knew he was loved for *who* he was, not *how* he was physically.

Other lessons concerning communication with doctors were a little harder for me to learn.

I didn't always provide timely information about changes in my husband's health or behavior. Most often, it was because I didn't understand the significance of a change or recognize patterns until they were fairly well developed. Except for any obvious critical concerns, there were so many things going on with EJ, I didn't know which ones merited reporting to the doctor and which were just normal, given his physical condition.

For example, I had not heard of "Sundowning Syndrome," although my husband had exhibited the symptoms for months. Briefly, the patient's confusion increases, and their state of mind appears to decline in the early evening or as the sun is setting. He often became more agitated, restless, and less cooperative during these times of the evening. He also wandered and tried to leave the house, as if searching for something. When questioned, he couldn't identify what he was looking for and just stated, "I've lost it. I need to find it."

I didn't understand what was happening, yet it took me a while before I thought it was worth mentioning to his doctor.

Once I better understood the condition, I became better able to provide for his needs and safety.

Other times, I'm sure that I clung to hope, somehow afraid that if I verbalized my fears, they might somehow come true. In retrospect, I realize that thinking made no sense. It was a form of superstition, but it still lingered in my thoughts.

I learned, in time, to be alert to changes, not worry about wasting the doctor's time and let them be the judge of what's important. Whenever I recognized them for what they were, I also quit entertaining harmful superstitious thoughts.

Repeatedly, I would have to make critical decisions concerning my husband's well-being and the impact on the family. Yet, since none of us has complete knowledge of the future, I could only pray I had gathered as much information as possible to make the best objective decision. These decisions were seldom easy, and I experienced a lot of stress while trying to sort it all out.

One of the most difficult situations arose after I received a call concerning a last minute, overseas work assignment.

My company was opening an ultra-luxury hotel in Jakarta. I received a four-day notice that I was needed at the hotel to assist with several high-level and time-sensitive personnel issues related to the opening. As the Vice President of Human Resources, I alone could fulfill these responsibilities. My presence and guidance were needed on site; there were no other alternatives available.

It was a push to make the arrangements for my departure, but as a family, we once again made the necessary preparations for my prolonged absence.

Two days before I was to leave, my husband experienced a frightening grand mal seizure. He was taken to the emergency room and later admitted for overnight observation. He was cleared to go home the next morning. Prior to his release, I met with the doctor to discuss the event and my husband's discharge from the hospital.

I had a very difficult decision to make.

I was the sole financial support of our family, and additionally, we needed my employer's benefit coverage to care for my husband. There was no one who could replace me in time to fulfill my responsibilities with the Jakarta project. A refusal to go would greatly impact the opening of the hotel, probably end my current employment, and ruin any prospects with other employers. Surprisingly, at a certain level, hospitality is essentially a small industry and professional reputations can be made or broken quite easily. A vice president is expected to show up for critical events within the company.

Several of my fellow executives were also patients of the doctor. He was very aware of my company's demands and my role within the organization. I provided him with an overview of my assignment, anticipated duration of the assignment, and the arrangements I'd made for my husband's care during my absence.

"I'm not asking you to make the decision; I'm asking you to share what I need to know to make the best decision I am able. I will have to live with the consequences of that decision," I explained to the doctor.

I hoped I sounded clear-headed and brave to the doctor. In truth, I felt anything but that.

The doctor stared intensely into my eyes as he took a few minutes to think about his response. When he spoke, it was with great seriousness, equaled by his deep compassion for us.

He explained that the grand mal seizure could be considered random. It was not a clear precursor to another serious event, and in fact, one may not occur again. He stated that my husband may recover well, but there was no way of knowing, nor any way of predicting if there'd be another event.

"No matter what, whether you're here or not, you cannot blame yourself if something happens. He may be fine for years to come," he stated as he firmly, yet briefly, squeezed my hand.

I sat in silence for a moment before thanking him for his help.

Later, and after much discussion as a family, we decided I should go forward with the trip to Indonesia. The "kids," actually now adults in their twenties, were prepared to handle any emergency that might occur. I thank God that EJ was in good, loving hands and didn't experience another critical event during my absence. I'm also grateful that my children didn't have to experience all that would have been required of them, under those circumstances.

STEPPINGSTONES

∾ Listen, listen, listen!

∾ Ask questions. Don't worry about letting others know I don't understand something. Take notes and keep them organized and the information easy to retrieve when needed.

∾ When making difficult decisions, gather as much information as possible, discuss the issues with those who can best guide me and include those who will be affected by my decision. Try to be objective and, ultimately, pray hard and just do the best I can.

That's all anyone can ask.

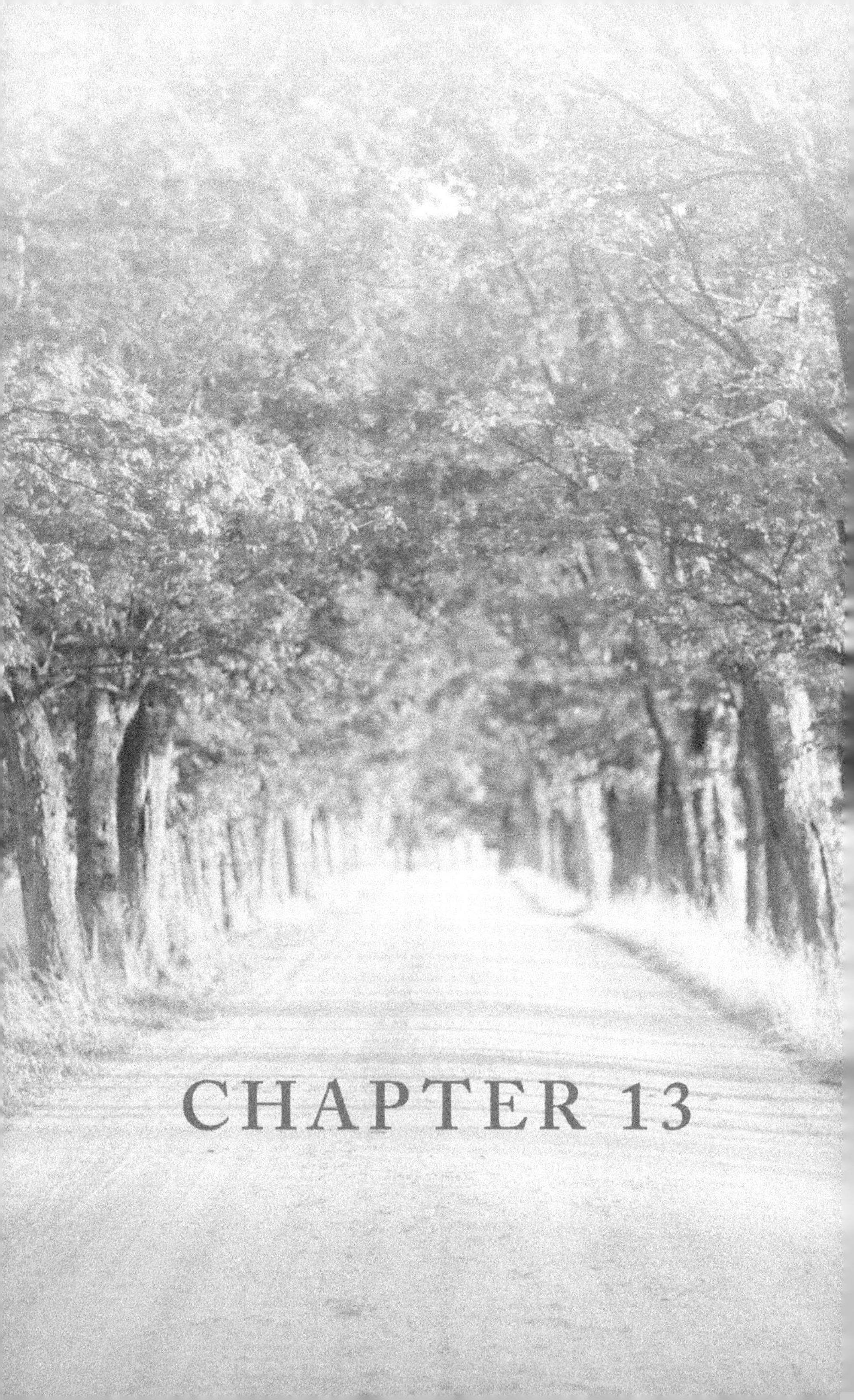

CHAPTER 13

Necessary Confrontations

You will know the truth, and the truth alone,
will make you free.
John 8:32

God is close to all of them that call upon him,
in truth.
Psalm 145:18

It's not enough to say the right things;
we must do the right things with love and honesty.
1John 3:18

Liars are abomination to the Lord; but they that
are truthful and honest in all their dealings,
are his delight.
Proverbs 12:22

I'm a "Navy Brat" who grew up in base housing and learned quite early that standing up to bullies is a necessary life skill. However, as an adult, I never expected the multiple times I would have to confront similar abhorrent behaviors.

Following EJ's stroke, I soon realized there are times when caregivers need to assert themselves, no matter how challenging this may be for them.

Unfortunately, I found this to be true on multiple occasions and, surprisingly, included encounters with family, doctors, neighbors, and others. How you approach these situations will vary, based upon the relationship and the power balance over the outcome for your loved one's care.

Ultimately, a caregiver must always find the courage and energy to stand firm for what's right and fair. After all, you are now in charge of making big decisions that will have a lasting impact on your loved one and your family.

When it's necessary to stand up for your rights, attack the issue, not the person. Be non-adversarial but firm. The power of recognizing the truth of the situation is enough for you to confront lies, bad intentions and apathy.

Armed with a selfless motive, you have the needed strength to tackle the issue before you.

It's sometimes difficult to not get caught up in the drama, take offense or feel overwhelmed by the obstacles blocking your progress. When I found myself approaching or falling into these traps, it was helpful to remember that some things aren't negotiable.

Truth is the only antidote to a lie; love is the only antidote to hate, and apathy can be countered by a swift kick in the pants. Well, there are better strategies available to you than giving someone the boot, but sometimes it took me a little bit of work to overcome that impulse.

At the very time you have the least energy or heart for battle, you may have no choice. Sometimes you may have to verbally wrestle with others just to do their job or give you the needed information, so you can do yours.

It's not fair, but it happens.

A starting point in building your arsenal of caregiver's weapons is to have at least a basic understanding of you and your loved one's rights and non-negotiables.

Family Matters

We've all heard the stories. "The true nature of people is revealed during a time of crisis."

This can be especially true within families.

Often, families come together during these times in extraordinary, selfless, and loving ways. Or, as in so many situations, family members may show an ugly, shameful side that hadn't been revealed before.

Our family experienced both.

In the blink of an eye, I had become not only the primary earner but also the sole financial support for the family. Thankfully, I was continually offered professional opportunities that, while more demanding, increased my earnings. Accepting these assignments was only possible because of the at-home support of my children.

It was a blessing beyond measure to have adult children, each in their twenties at the time, willing and able to help, no matter their own circumstances. In turn, each of them stepped away from their personal lives, including school, sweethearts, and work, to care for EJ in my absence.

This was no small feat, especially during the first year he was home. At that point, my husband still needed help with all of the basic functions of life. Thankfully, Tom, the oldest son, took the year off from his own life to assume the majority of these very personal care responsibilities. At six feet five inches tall, extremely fit, and undaunting in the face of adversity, Tom was the perfect one to care for EJ's needs during this very difficult phase of recovery. When his time as a caregiver ended, Tom joined the Coast Guard; it was a perfect match with his humanitarian nature.

As EJ's level of needed care changed throughout the following years, both Lynn and John assisted with these responsibilities and even became the primary caregivers when I was required to travel for work.

Lynn, who is fiercely protective and yet possesses the most tender of hearts and infinite patience, took over from Tom. There is no middle ground with Lynn, it is her nature to approach everything with great passion. Only later did I realize that her innate kindness and capacity to demonstrate love in so many ways were critical to both my husband's survival and my own. We could not have made it through those difficult years, without her many sacrifices.

John, no longer a teenager with shaggy ginger-colored hair, had grown into an exceptional young man. He lived with us for years to assist with the care of my husband. He too was tall and fit, but it is his character that made him suited for his new responsibilities. Throughout that time, he demonstrated immense caring, compassion, and dedication, always putting our needs above his own. His wit, if not his endless practical jokes, made life so much more bearable. We relied upon his help, and he gave it willingly.

All three have chosen to live their lives in service to others, as do their wives. We are all better for their commitment and efforts.

How blessed am I to be a part of their family!

Some have expressed their surprise that my children would put their own relationships, education, and careers aside for a minimum of a year to care for a stepfather.

I don't know how to respond to that. EJ wasn't perfect, and neither were the kids or I, for that matter. But there was—and still is—a bond of love, loyalty and devotion that overcomes everything else. To this day, I am humbled by their years of personal sacrifice and service to the family, and my gratitude can never be overstated.

I hope all caregivers have the love and as much support from their families as they need.

Sadly, as I was to learn, it's not uncommon to have to deal with surprising behaviors of some family members during extremely trying times.

Greed surfaced repeatedly in ours. At the time of his release, my husband could barely understand the world around him, was immobile and struggled to speak in the most basic terms. Yet, it was at this time that some visiting relatives with their own self-interests chose to make their moves. It was as if these people smelled blood in the water and wanted to grab their share of the carcass before it was gone.

One afternoon, I came upon someone trying to get my husband to sign a fake document concerning a loan of $5,000. It was backdated, included an interest rate, which was pulled out of the air, and other repayment terms. Fortunately, EJ didn't recognize what this relative was attempting to accomplish and innocently called out for me to help him sign the document.

Needless to say, the transaction did not proceed.

On another occasion soon after EJ's initial release from the hospital, I came upon another family member trying to persuade a teenage relative to go talk with my husband, alone. In a conspiratorial tone, I overheard the coaching on how to get him to commit to buying a car for the teen. Both were startled when I made my presence known.

The discussion did not go any further.

On an entirely separate issue, I was crushed and felt abandoned when my parents refused to travel to be with me during the first critical weeks following EJ's stroke. No matter my pleading, each request was met with a very sincere apology followed by a definite "no".

Too long afterward, I discovered that my parents were concealing their own medical issues from me. Within six months of each other, both passed away from cancer. I learned far too late that what I had believed to be a lack of support in my greatest hour of need, was an attempt to shield me from further grief.

They were, in fact, demonstrating their love for me in the way they thought best.

I should have trusted my parents more; I should have felt comforted and loved no matter my disappointment at not having them physically near me.

I have regrets about my own parenting. This is especially true during the time following EJ's massive stroke. In retrospect, much like my own parents, my efforts to shield my children from pain didn't have the desired outcome. I now believe my actions caused them to suffer more. It was devastating for me to learn years later how some of my decisions impacted them.

Each of them sacrificed so much in their personal lives to support EJ and me. Additionally, they too experienced a sense of great loss, sadness, and fear. I wasn't there for them as EJ's issues and the struggle to keep us all afloat demanded the majority of my focus, at the time. Yet, they soldiered on and continued to give more than should ever be expected of children.

I would give anything to have a do-over.

The biggest problem was that I wasn't transparent about things that mattered to them. I miscalculated their ability to handle the information I withheld from them, and it hurt them in a variety of ways. Much like my own parents' dealings with me, my motive was to spare them further heartache. However, the choice to withhold difficult issues from my children left them on their own to wrongly interpret events. They suffered greatly, without me knowing of their pain until years later.

I wish I had listened more, paid attention to their silence more and done more to make them feel safe and loved.

I didn't make the time; I didn't have the words.

Amazingly, somehow, they love me, despite my shortcomings.

Transparency Matters

As with many young men at the time, EJ served in the Vietnam War. He was a member of the Air Force and "boots on the ground in Nam." Our neighbor, also a veteran, alerted me that my husband may be eligible for benefits through the Veteran's Administration. He cautioned that being approved for coverage would be a very long process but well worth the effort.

Naively, I thought "long process" meant a few months of effort on my part. I was wrong; it took years of awaiting appointments, eventually securing doctor's visits, and overcoming repeated administrative hurdles, many of them contradictory to the prior demands.

Clearly, the process was broken. Many times, I was tempted to just give up, but I didn't; there was too much at stake.

As it has been explained to me, the VA requires assessments by several different intake specialists and doctors to determine the patient's eligibility for benefits. Early in the process, one of the staff explained to me this was necessary because of the many attempted fraudulent claims. He further added that the goal was to weed out these people as early as possible. Unfortunately, that also meant that several people with legitimate claims couldn't navigate their way through the multi-layered system.

VA appointments of any type were hard to come by, and I was cautioned against being late, canceling, or missing appointments. We always arrived early, yet consistently waited long past the appointed time, to be seen.

This particular visit was, yet again, to assess EJ's mental health status. At this point in time, his dementia and Parkinson's had greatly increased.

The day began no differently than our prior experiences. We were early and waited in a very crowded area along with other patients. Seating was limited and completely full, so I stood next to my husband's wheelchair. He was happy to be around other veterans and tried to converse with them. Eventually, I interrupted his cheerful chatter with a fellow Viet Nam Vet to let him know I was going to the restroom.

While waiting for the restroom to become vacant, I wandered a small bit down the back hallway. There, I came across a bulletin board which featured a large poster explaining "Patient's Rights." I found the poster interesting to read.

Everything seemed to be fairly common sense, but I was surprised to read that the patient had the right to have a family member or other designated person present during doctor's visits. I'd never thought of that before. I just assumed it was the right of the patient to include whomever they chose to be included in the visit.

I'd always been present during EJ's appointments. My presence had proven to be a great help for everyone, doctors included, so I didn't think much more about the poster as I returned to the waiting room area.

By a stroke of luck, I had excellent timing.

"Mr. Allen," called the doctor in a flat, bored tone of voice.

The doctor's white coat landed barely above the hem of her mini skirt. I didn't like that or the platform tennis shoes she wore, nor the way she looked above the crowd and wrinkled her nose as if she smelled an offensive odor.

"We're here," I called and began pushing my husband's wheelchair toward her.

"You're not allowed in. I will see the patient alone," she bluntly responded.

"Doctor, I won't be in the way, I promise. I know that he is the patient, and you need to speak directly with him. But others have found it very helpful to have me nearby to assist if he gets anxious or confused. I'd like to accompany him."

"I'm not comfortable with that. I can manage him. Please stay here," she said as she moved toward the wheelchair.

I stepped forward to body-block her progress toward the wheelchair's handles. "Doctor, I'm most comfortable when the rights of the patient and his family are honored. I just read them on your bulletin board. Perhaps I misunderstood the guidelines. Should we go read them together?"

She gave me what is commonly known as "the hairy eyeball" before turning and brusquely saying over her shoulder, "Follow me."

Throughout the consultation, EJ was in a great mood but often refused to answer the doctor's questions in English. Instead, he chose to respond in his beloved first language, French. This started with the first, standard question, "Do you know today's date?"

The doctor wasn't pleased with his answer in French and asked him to repeat his response in English. He complied and continued to speak English while answering her next few questions.

However, when she directed him to count backwards from one hundred by sevens, he reverted to French. She stopped him and again asked him to speak English. He did so for a little while but slipped back into French when he arrived at sixty-five. Exasperated, the doctor begrudgingly gave up on the counting exercise.

She asked a few more questions, to which he would randomly respond in either English or French. He responded appropriately each time she asked for a translation but seemed puzzled about her requests.

I sat silently observing their exchanges; it was obvious the doctor was becoming more frustrated with each French response. And it was obvious to me that my husband didn't notice her attitude.

Finally, she asked him to write a sentence. He paused quite a while and stared at the ceiling in deep thought. We all sat in silence, until eventually EJ smiled at me and then wrote, "La vie en rose et je t'aime beaucoup."

After first showing me the note, he slid it toward the doctor.

"I told you; I don't speak French!" she angrily barked at him.

"Are you sure? It's so beautiful, you should try it," he earnestly responded.

The doctor was now ready to speak with me directly. She asked me to translate the note and had several other questions about changes in my husband's mental health. Responding to each of her requests, I was able to give her an accurate description of his generally happy disposition, but declining mental and physical abilities.

The visit ended with a referral to see the next level of physician for further evaluation.

In the VA world, that's considered a very good thing.

Dignity and
Respect Matter

Our little neighborhood diner was always busy, but especially so on Saturday mornings.

At this point, EJ was able to use a walker to go short distances and enjoyed people-watching along the way. While it took some assistance on my part to get my husband up and down from the stools at the counter, watching all the hustle and bustle of the kitchen activity made it well worth the effort.

Our usual order was a stack of pancakes and a cup of coffee strong enough to make your hair curl. Sometimes EJ left his food untouched. On other occasions, he'd ask for a double order, unaware of how much he'd already eaten. I didn't care or try to reason with him in either case; I just wanted him happy and went with the flow.

During one of our outings, I overheard the man next to my husband asking a lot of personal questions about his stroke and disabilities. Running interference, I quickly introduced myself and began asking questions of him. He explained that he was a neurologist, new in town and believed he could help with my husband's recovery.

Hope sprang anew for me, and I asked for his card. I promised to call for an appointment the following week.

I followed through and got the earliest available appointment. Although the doctor was out of network for our benefit plans, I didn't hesitate to pay for the expensive visit in full.

On the day of the appointment, my husband seemed to be struggling with a lot of confusion and anxiety. It took great effort to get him ready and dressed for the visit. In one sense, I thought it was a good thing for the doctor to evaluate him on one of EJ's "off days" and make his recommendations accordingly.

Upon our arrival at the doctor's office, we were greeted warmly and asked to wait in a pleasant examination room. The doctor joined us very quickly, greeted me and reintroduced himself to EJ. My husband ignored the doctor's extended hand and just stared at him.

"What, you don't remember me?" the doctor asked. I thought his comment was an attempt at humor. Upon reflection, I suspect that his ego may have been bruised.

EJ gave me a bewildered look. I reminded him that we'd met the doctor before and spoke about his role to help him with the progression of his recovery. EJ critically looked the doctor up and down without saying a word. Clearly, he wasn't impressed.

It was not a good start to the visit.

The doctor began his examination but, oddly, directed his questions to me rather than my husband, the actual patient. Throughout the evaluation, he continued to make side comments about my husband to me.

EJ appeared increasingly stressed and confused by the situation. My heart ached for him; it was very difficult to witness their exchanges.

"Watch this, he won't be able to answer this question," the doctor said at one point, as he winked at me in a conspiratorial manner.

"Thank you, doctor. You're right, he won't be answering. We're finished." I'd had enough and turned to my husband.

"Sweetheart, you don't need to answer any more questions. It's time for us to go." Gathering our things, I wheeled my husband to the front desk and paid the extraordinarily high bill before leaving.

Even though I was terribly upset, I couldn't ignore that it was a lovely day in our little neighborhood. I navigated my husband's wheelchair down the tree-lined sidewalk leading to the parking lot.

"Wait, wait, Mrs. Allen, Mrs. Allen!" I heard the call behind me and stopped to see the doctor hurrying to catch up with us.

He rapidly acknowledged his lack of respect for my husband and apologized for his conduct. He handed me several booklets about strokes and other resources for useful information. He apologized repeatedly and then asked if I'd give him another chance to help my husband.

"Thank you, but no," I firmly responded without hesitation and wished him a good day.

No one capable of that level of disrespect deserved a second chance to bully someone who can't fight back.

Never tolerate a lack of respect and dignity toward your loved one or yourself.

Truth Matters

We were now two and a half years into the VA benefit claims process, with no determination regarding my husband's status/disability rating. It had been a long journey to get to this point, as evidenced by the more than five feet of kitchen counter space filled with boxes of chronologically ordered correspondence between the VA and me.

At last, we received an appointment with the doctor to make the final recommendations regarding EJ's eligibility for benefits. I'd been informed we were to be the last appointment of the day. As usual, I left work early to ensure we wouldn't be late.

The few "Disabled Parking" spots were completely filled, and I needed to park a long way from the hospital entrance. It took a long time to walk the distance with him, and although today he was using a cane, his progress towards the building was even slower than normal. We both felt the full force of the late afternoon Florida sun as we crossed the huge, steamy, asphalt parking lot.

Thankfully, once inside, another Vet was leaving the building and offered up his wheelchair. It was a Godsend, as I pushed EJ's wheelchair through the big building, hurriedly tried to navigate the hallways and find our appointment at the other end of the expansive hospital.

EJ and I were both worn out from the heat and the effort it took to find the correct office. Yet somehow, we arrived right on time.

"Mr. Allen?" the grumpy doctor asked, within moments of our arrival.

"We're here, Sir," I responded.

The doctor didn't offer either of us a greeting and, in fact, seemed quite perturbed by something. He glanced at my husband, before turning back to me and saying the now familiar phrase, "I prefer to meet with the patient alone."

"We prefer staying together. I think that's our right, isn't it?" I smiled, sincerely hoping to avoid a confrontation but ready for one if needed. Unfortunately, as the saying goes, this wasn't my first rodeo.

"All right. But if he can walk with a cane, the wheelchair stays here."

"Doctor, he's tired. It will go much faster if he can stay in the wheelchair. Please reconsider."

"No, there isn't room in the office for both of you and the wheelchair. You decide which it will be." And with that, the doctor turned to walk down the lengthy hall.

I helped my husband to his feet, handed him his cane, and we began to follow the doctor, who was now several yards ahead of us. As he continued down the long hallway, he turned occasionally to see where we were. Each time he observed our lack of progress, he shook his head, as if disgusted by our delay.

By the time we arrived at the examination room, the doctor was already seated behind a small table. On the wall directly behind him, was a large calendar with the date clearly circled by red magnetic rings. He directed each of us where we were to sit across from him.

Before beginning his examination, the doctor gave me very stern instructions that I was not to speak or interfere with the examination. It was hard to interpret his tone as anything other than rude and condescending. I was surprised, but not ruffled.

"Mr. Allen, please tell me today's date," the doctor instructed EJ.

"I can, if you move your head just a little," he replied and pointed to the calendar with a red circle around the current date. "You put that there to help me, right?" Although EJ was experiencing increasing dementia, he was no fool.

The doctor was not amused and continued with the examination.

By now, EJ was very familiar with the variety of questions asked to determine the status of his mental health. Today, he elected to respond in English; evidently, he was in no mood to encourage this doctor to learn French.

I sat silently while the appointment progressed. There were several times my husband seemed anxious, was confused by the questions, and looked to me for help. I knew he'd gotten several answers wrong and also noted the doctor's attitude when this happened.

It appeared to me the doctor believed EJ was faking some of his responses. I knew this was not the case. Yet, true to my word, I said nothing to EJ, other than to reassure him that everything was all right and he should just do the best he could. That would be enough, I assured him.

Finally, the doctor ended the examination.

"Mrs. Allen, your husband is fine. There's nothing wrong that's outside of the normal range," the doctor said, staring down at his notes to avoid looking me in the eye as he spoke.

He was lying. I knew it, and he knew that I knew it.

Separate from the VA, several other doctors were tracking EJ's seriously declining mental state and the onset of Parkinson's. Yet, this doctor was going to make the lone contrary evaluation that would impact our lives forever, hiding under the guise of his supposedly "objective, professional judgment."

I understood the situation well and was both calm and confident that the simple truth would eventually prevail. My only job at that moment was to illustrate the truth of EJ's physical status to the doctor.

"Doctor, I've witnessed everything in silence. However, I'd now like to ask my husband one question. Is that all right with you?" I said respectfully.

"Go ahead, as long as it's just one question." He begrudgingly indulged me, while looking at his watch.

"Sweetheart, I want to ask you a question, and I need you to tell me the truth. First, before you answer I want you to know that you will not hurt my feelings in any way." I looked deeply into EJ's eyes as I continued. "And no one is going to be upset with your answer. Is it okay if I ask you that question?"

"Okay," he responded nervously.

"Honey, how old do you think I am?" I waited for the answer while EJ paused for a few minutes and looked around the room, as if the correct answer was posted somewhere, just like the calendar.

"EJ, it's okay; you won't hurt my feelings. Sweetheart, how old do you think I am?"

"You promise you won't be upset if I think you're older than you really are?" he asked.

"I promise. How old do you think I am?"

"Thirty-four?" he said, with a great deal of hesitation.

"Thank you, My Love. That's very kind." It was now the doctor's turn to sit in silence, observing us. My next question was for him.

"Doctor, please, I'd like for you to go on record with how old you think I am."

"Mrs. Allen, I couldn't say."

"First, before I answer, I want you to know that my husband deserves to get every penny of the benefits he's entitled to, but not one penny more. And secondly, Doctor, thank you for not guessing my age. You might have hurt my feelings. For the record, I'm sixty-one."

"Liar! J'accuse!!!" EJ's deep, incredulous laugh as he pointed at me revealed that he still believed his original assessment of my age to be true. Continuing to point at me, he then turned and said, "Doctor, I think she's the one who's crazy, don't you? You better put that in your notes. But don't take her away; she's my crazy person."

That did it; the floodgates opened.

The tension in the room ended, as the three of us shared our unrestrained laughter and enjoyed these moments together.

Very relaxed now, EJ began to give his new friend the benefit of his opinions concerning a variety of topics, including, of course, how the French have been deeply misrepresented throughout history. While speaking, he slipped easily between English and French, never imagining the doctor might not understand him. The doctor gave no indication that he had any problem following EJ's lectures in either language. He also now seemed to have all the time in the world to listen to my husband's stories and engage in pleasant conversation with him.

At last, EJ announced that he was tired and told the doctor it was time for him to go home and have a cold beer or more, to be followed by a long "snoozatunity."

I was pleasantly surprised when the doctor locked up the office and continued to talk with my husband about "shoes and ships and sealing wax, cabbages and kings," as he walked with us all the way back to our car. The doctor kindly offered to push EJ's wheelchair, but I declined his offer. Not wanting to interfere with the great time they both were having; I spoke very little as we progressed toward the car.

Before bidding the doctor, "*Au revoir*," EJ invited him to stop by the house anytime to share a few beers. We all shook hands and went on our way.

I was so grateful for the way the visit turned out, yet I had no idea about the outcome of the doctor's final report. My only expectation was that he would be truthful in recording his findings.

That was good enough for me.

Once home, the evening ended as it often did, with a late dinner. EJ alternated between drinking a cold Heineken and eating a Klondike ice cream bar as we rocked on the porch and watched the fireworks from nearby Disney World.

I thanked God for such a love-filled life. I still do.

Back at work the next day, I was very surprised to get a call from the doctor we had just met with yesterday. Usually, that wouldn't be a good omen. However, my apprehension quickly dissipated as he explained the reason for his call.

"Mrs. Allen, I couldn't sleep last night, thinking about meeting you and your husband. I've never seen such devotion and love before. I can only pray that if my wife and I are ever put to the test, our love will be enough to meet our challenges. Our meeting yesterday was such a blessing and has changed the way I will work with patients going forward. I just want to say thank you, sincerely thank you. I just had to let you know how I feel."

I shared with the doctor how I was deeply grateful, touched and humbled by his words. I wished him well and thanked him for his very important work and service to others. We did not speak about the outcome of his evaluation; it wasn't the point of his call.

Afterward, I expressed my gratitude to God that we'd all had such an uplifting experience. We never encountered the doctor again, but I trust that he remained diligent in his work, while demonstrating a more thoughtful and understanding heart toward others in his care.

It would be several months before I learned of the doctor's official evaluation. It was honest, fair, and made a real difference in our lives and the benefits we received.

Thank God.

Privacy Matters

Be prepared to protect yourself and your family members from overly curious, misguided, or ill-intentioned people.

You may be surprised by the number of curious neighbors, coworkers and other individuals who suddenly have a deep interest in your personal affairs. Contrary to what they may claim as the source of their concerns, often they are motivated by a deeper, morbid interest that has nothing to do with the welfare of your family members.

It's shameful behavior, but as I learned all too soon, some people have no shame.

I became especially and painfully aware of this during another critical medical event of my husband's. He'd suffered another grand mal seizure while preparing for his shower. He collapsed on the bathroom floor and was naked, hallucinating and violently thrashing. It was terrifying and heart-wrenching to witness.

The 911 operator determined a Medivac operation was required to get him to the needed level of critical care facility. Fortunately, our home was three doors down from a large soccer field where the helicopter was able to land safely. The noisy landing in the midst of our normally quiet residential area created a lot of curiosity. Many people rushed over to get a glimpse of the activities.

Soon, our bedroom and bathroom were jammed with first responders and other personnel attending to my husband. I was asked to give them room to treat him but stayed nearby in the next room. I hovered by the door, deep in prayer for his well-being. The house was so noisy and bustling with people in a variety of uniforms, that it was difficult to remain focused.

"Mrs. Allen! Mrs. Allen! Do you know these people?" a policeman called loudly to me over the commotion.

Searching through the crowd, I eventually realized he was speaking about the couple at his side. Somehow, they had wriggled their way into the very area where the EMTs were working on my husband.

"No, sir, I do not!" I responded.

In a very firm manner, the officer then escorted the couple out of the house. As they were hustled past me, the man smirked and hurriedly claimed, "Although we've never met, we're concerned neighbors from down the way."

He was right about one thing—I'd never seen them before. Nor, thankfully, did I ever see them again.

Some people have no boundaries.

On another day, I might have confronted these disgusting people, but at the time, I had three other pressing concerns: my husband's welfare, covering his nakedness as they rolled him out on the stretcher, and since I'd been told there wasn't room in the helicopter for me, how would I get to the hospital where they were taking him?

Accountability Matters

Sadly, it is very likely that along the way, you will encounter an administrator who just doesn't care about their job, your needs or the consequences of their decision not to fulfill their responsibilities.

When I encountered these individuals, I quickly evaluated the best way to confront their behavior and achieve my desired results from our interactions. Generally, my strategic options were engagement, accountability or using the chain of command.

Depending upon the specific circumstances, I sometimes needed to employ a combination of strategies to overcome a temporary obstacle created by another's lack of concern or competence.

Engagement

Is it productive to attempt to engage the person in your case? Sometimes, the grinding nature of their work can cause even good, dedicated administrators to temporarily "check out" and forget that service is a part of their jobs. If this is the case, there's a chance to gain their interest in your situation and needs. It's worth trying to revive their better nature and sense of duty.

Call the person by name, thank them for their help (in advance of it actually being demonstrated), don't waste their time with chit-chat, but do tell them your concerns and ask if there is other information that you need to know.

And finally, be sure to clarify what you've agreed upon and their recommended next steps or actions.

Engaging the other person was the strategy that proved most successful for me. Very often, the person completely reversed a "burned-out attitude" and became extremely helpful. Some, especially at the VA, even offered up "insider tips" to navigating the very complex and layered system they had to deal with on a daily basis.

I considered these conversions from apathy to engagement victories for all involved. But there were also other added dividends; the administrator experienced a refreshed attitude, and my husband benefited from their help.

Engagement is a win-win.

Accountability

When it's evident that engagement won't work as the first choice, you need to ramp up your strategy.

Pleasantly, let the person know you're taking notes for your later reference/reminder of the conversation. Ask the spelling of their name, then verbally confirm the time and date of your conversation.

Generally, my conversations would go something like this:

"Before we go further, I'd like for you to know that I'm taking notes of our conversation so that I don't overlook or forget something that we've covered today.

May I have the spelling of your name, please?

Thanks, let's check that we have the same date and time.

Got it. Now, may I have your direct phone number, just in case we get disconnected, or I need to follow up with you?

And, just in case I can't reach you, what's the name and direct line for your supervisor?

Great, many thanks for that! Here's why I'm calling you today . . ."

Cowardly or just plain lazy people often wake up at this point and realize someone will hold them accountable for their behavior. They may not sincerely care to help you, but they have been put on notice that you will follow up if they don't do their job or they give you inaccurate information.

These folks are not entitled to your full confidence.

Put a trace date in your calendar and be sure to follow up and check that the actions they committed to doing are, in fact, completed.

Chain of Command

There are some people who are quite willing to be an obstacle to your progress. Sadly, there are also some who feel more powerful by making others feel more helpless. Don't put up with these counterproductive and offensive actions and don't waste your time trying to negotiate with those who behave this way.

Do not be intimidated by bullying, rude, or incompetent individuals.

You need correct information, forms completed correctly and a clear understanding of any needed actions concerning pending items.

You deserve respect and professionalism with each exchange; and frankly, it's their job to provide these.

I checked my own motives before responding to people in this category. It didn't always work, but I tried to ask myself, was I being unreasonable, demanding or overly sensitive? While I wasn't exactly objective about my own behavior, I tried to assess it through another's eyes.

Following a few incidents, I had to acknowledge that I was the one having a meltdown over one more duplicate—no triplicate—administrative issue. I was exhausted by the effort required to complete what should be routine tasks.

I had come ready for combat, and I found it. However, my behavior wasn't helpful and, in fact, wasted a lot of energy and time. Additionally, I needed to repair the damage my runaway mouth had created and attempt to re-engage others to help me.

However, that wasn't generally the case, and there are certain situations where you must assert yourself to get the treatment you and your loved one deserve. If you encounter someone who is determined to block your efforts, go straight to the supervisor.

Everyone has a boss, and you have the right to ask to speak with that person. When you connect with that person, be calm while explaining the situation. Do so accurately and without added drama. Be concise about what you are trying to accomplish and address any pending questions or concerns before ending the conversation. Share accurately what the subordinate's response was that prompted you to request to speak with someone of higher authority. Take notes including the name, title, and direct contact information of the supervisor.

If you are still not satisfied with the outcome of your discussion, ask to speak with the next level of authority.

Although going up the chain of command was my least favorite strategy, I had to employ it a few times, particularly in long-term care facilities. However reluctant I was to engage in conflict, I realized that avoidance would never lead to resolution.

In each case, eventually, all our issues were resolved but sometimes required more persistence on my part than should have been required.

It once took me several attempts to secure an appointment and four onsite visits to the Navy base to get a military I.D. card renewed. This updated I.D. is critical to military personnel and their dependents. Visits required an appointment which took weeks to secure. Each trip meant I had to take time off work. Each time I met with a different person who informed me that contrary to the earlier instructions I'd been given, yet a different document was needed to complete the process.

I understood the first requests because our circumstances were a little unusual. EJ was once again in the hospital and unable to accompany me, the dependent. I complied with the request for photos from his hospital bed, but upon returning to the base, was told they needed to be notarized. Although during the prior visits I had asked, "Is there anything else that is needed?" each return visit concluded with an additional layer of administrative requests.

After being turned away the fourth time, I finally asked to speak with the officer in charge. He treated me with complete respect and courtesy. I explained our special circumstances and reviewed the long list of requests from his office. Without further discussion, he personally stepped behind the counter, took my picture, and issued the I.D. cards.

He apologized for my treatment and explained that the task should have been completed in one visit. The officer stated that those working the desk were not the normal staff, and he would ensure they got the training they needed to better serve others in the future.

I appreciated his authentic apology and was thankful to have the issue resolved at last.

STEPPINGSTONES

∾ Be transparent with those I love and ask for the same in return. No matter how painful, we can bear the truth together.

∾ Protect my loved ones from those with self-serving agendas. Forgive the aggressors, but don't allow them to hurt us any further. Confront issues, not people. The truth will always prevail.

∾ Know our rights to fair, honest, and respectful treatment.

∾ Hold my ground. I have the strength through God to know what's true and to do what's right.

CHAPTER 14

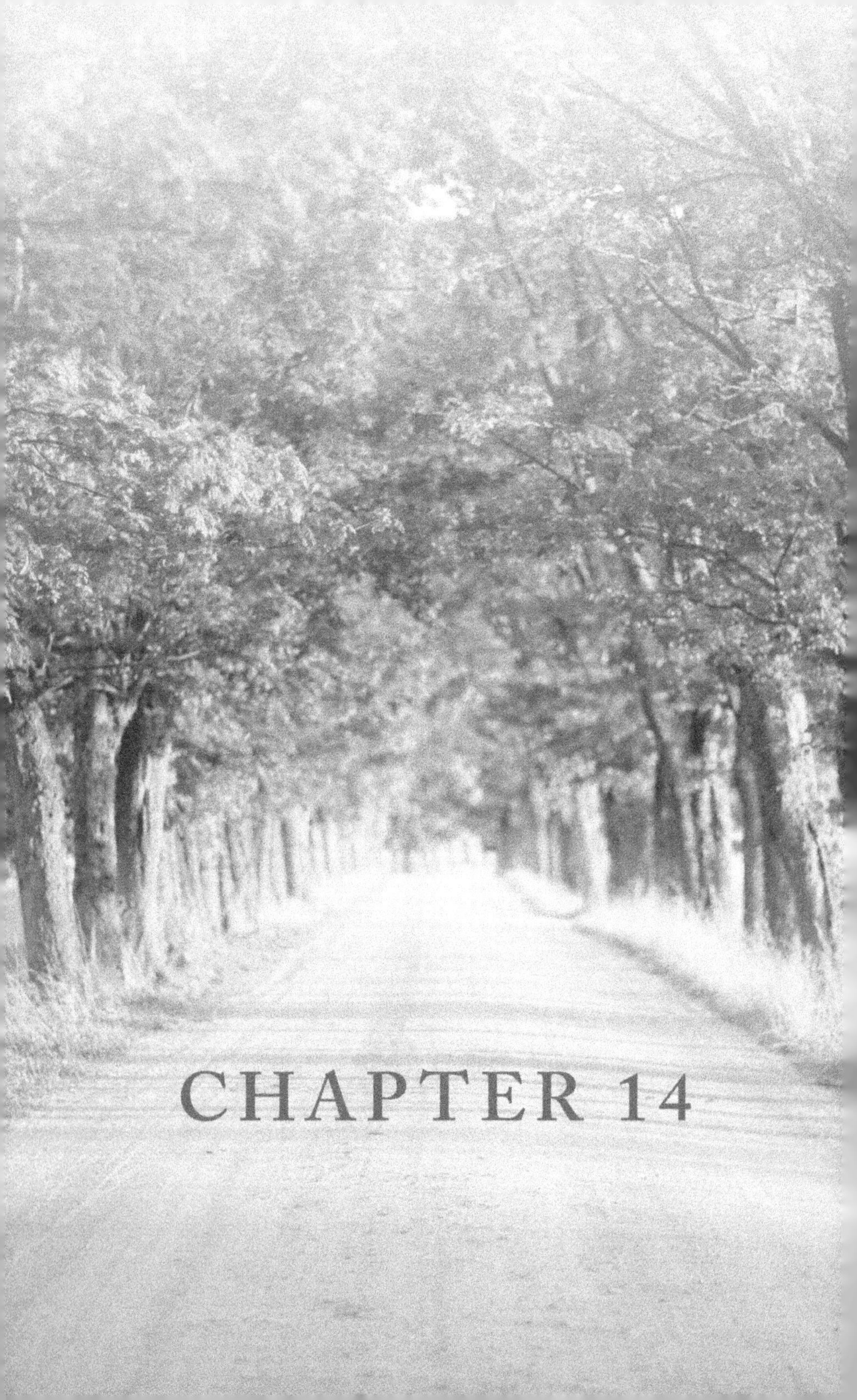

Juggling Chainsaws, while Riding a Unicycle, Atop a High Wire

What Could Possibly Go Wrong?

Increasingly, I began to understand that the demands upon me were not going to diminish. In fact, they seemed to snowball more rapidly as time progressed.

My purpose, as I saw it, was to just try to take care of my family, my job, and maybe—just maybe—myself. Balancing and fulfilling my responsibilities to my family and my employer were non-negotiables. The reason for this was simple: they counted on me. Nothing in these realms of my accountabilities could be traded away, nor could I opt out of what was required of me. I had to do my duty. Taking care of myself was much less of a priority.

It didn't matter that I felt inadequate, exhausted, and sometimes unreasonably angry at my husband, God, and others, including strangers. I had to keep juggling and ensuring all my orbs of accountability remained in balance.

I had no choice. One slip, one miss, one fall and all these worlds, much like a long line of dominoes, would come tumbling down. I was terrified that my family would never recover from such devastation.

Worry and fear became my constant companions—something I'd seldom experienced in the pre-stroke years. Around others, I constantly tried to hide what was going on and fake my feelings. I really don't know if I was successful.

Regardless, I showed up and did my job.

Some days were better than others. Often the good days didn't last long. It wasn't unusual that, if I at last experienced some happiness or a moment of relaxation, I'd suddenly be interrupted by the jarring thought I'd forgotten some critical appointment, conversation, or other responsibility.

Worse yet, my fears often proved to be right.

Seemingly, there was no longer space in my life to fully experience contentment, peace, and trust in the possibility of positive outcomes for our family.

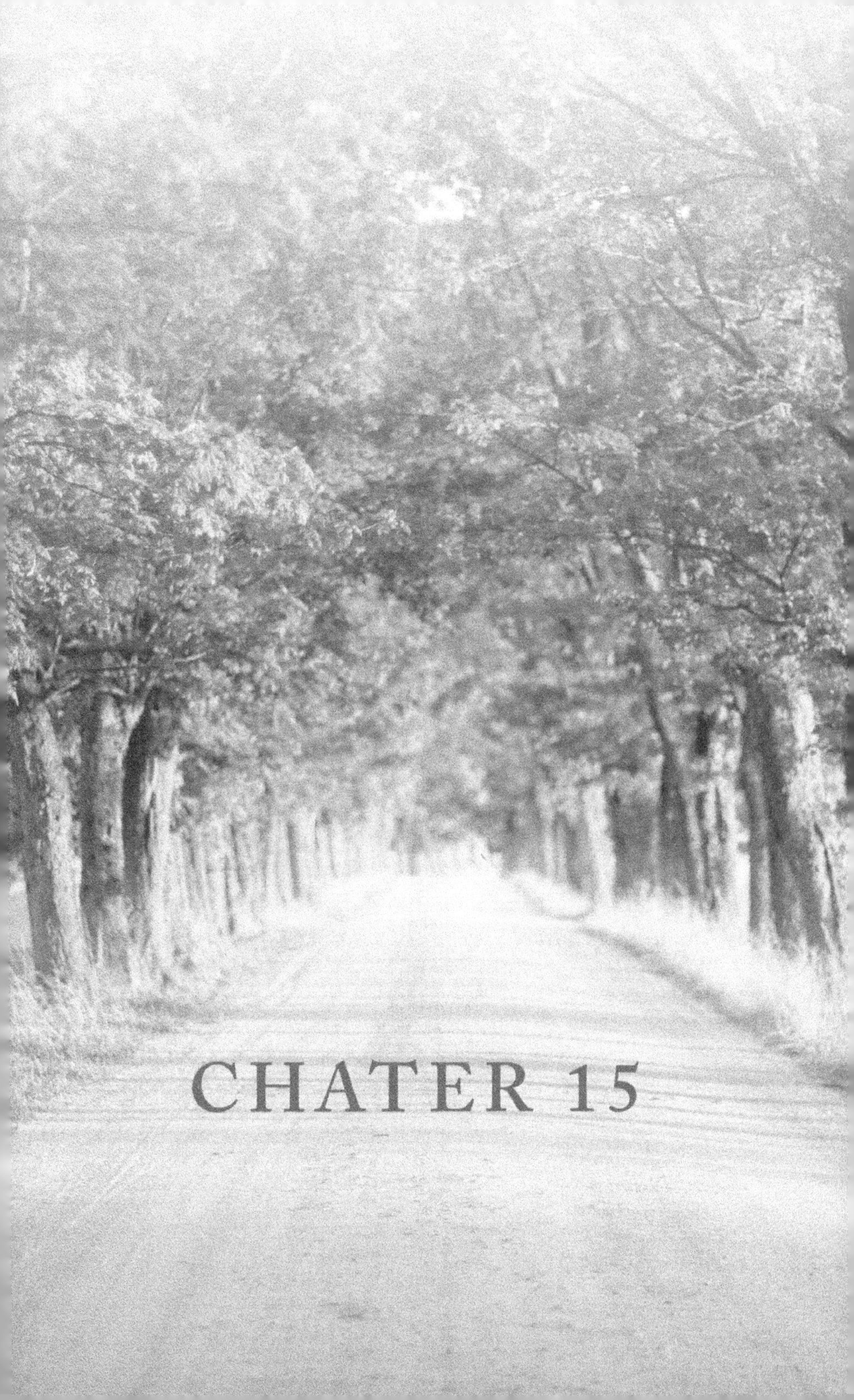

CHATER 15

When the Caregiver Needs Care

*In the Lord I put my trust. Sometimes this is very
hard, but ultimately, I always submit and renew
my trust in him. I have no other choice; he is God.*
Psalm 11:1

*Say to those who are afraid, "Be strong, our God
is already here and knows what we need,
He will save us."*
Isaiah 35:4

*When you pass through the waters, remember
I am with you. You will be safe, and the rivers
shall not overtake you. Likewise, when you walk
through the fire, you will be safe; you will not be
burned. You are mine and I will not forget you.*
Isaiah 43:2

*I am broken, my heart is shattered.
I'm being deconstructed, one splintering shard at a time.
I'm losing my identity; I'm losing ME, and I'm drowning in the broken pieces of a life that's not my own or of
my making.*

I need a lifeline, but I don't even have the strength to call for help.

Lies! Each one of these random thoughts was a lie and had no sustained power over me.

Yet, these very compelling thoughts often emerged from the shadows, deep in my imaginings, at the darkest moments in the night. My struggles between hopelessness and my ability to cope with each day's requirements seemed most intense when I was exhausted. Unfortunately, this was increasingly frequent.

Thankfully, these troubling ideas often dissipated with the arrival of dawn. Usually, I was able to begin the new day with a prayer of gratitude and praise. I embraced renewed hope for healing and guidance.

Then, I shifted my focus to the business of the day.

It wasn't until much later that I came to understand my sporadic experiences with depression, negative self-image and my feelings of hopelessness, anger and guilt weren't uncommon for caregivers. As sad as it was, it helped me to know I wasn't alone; I wasn't losing my mind. At least, I didn't think so.

Although many caregivers experience a new sense of purpose and reward from making a difference in the life of another, fulfilling their commitments requires a tremendous amount of energy and emotional stamina. These needed qualities aren't always easy to sustain.

Caregivers spend so much of their time giving of themselves, they often consider their own needs as the last priority. Along the way, they may experience frustration, depression, loss of their own identity, a sense of inadequacy, anger, and impatience—followed by deep feelings of guilt and regret. They can also experience joy, hope, faith, and a deep connection to God.

These highs can be dizzying, the lows desperately bleak. At least, that was my experience.

If you're able to see through their brave fronts, you may see the very caregivers you think of as such strong people may instead be in deep need of your empathy, compassion and, most especially, encouragement.

As with most caregivers, I was the last to know I needed help.

I was then and continue to be a very healthy person, without a history of physical complaints. Yet, within a few months of EJ's hospitalization, I realized things were changing with me.

One day, I awoke with an intense, persistent headache and tooth pain. I wasn't too alarmed since I was also having nightmares and woke up frequently throughout the night screaming. I thought my pain was just the result of lack of sleep. However, a prescheduled annual dental checkup revealed I had cracked two back molars, caused by clenching my jaw too hard in my sleep. A sleep guard and a little repair work on the teeth eliminated the headaches.

More than once, I noticed small, sore, crescent shaped, bloody marks on my palms. They were not deep and looked more like little scratches. At first, I ignored them, but when they continued to reappear, I began investigating the cause. While I was trying to figure out their origin, I made a lightly closed fist with one hand. I realized the bloody marks matched the shapes of my nail tips and were evidently caused by too tightly clenching my fists in my sleep.

At bedtime, the simple, preventive remedy was to roll up a pair of EJ's thick athletic socks and wear them like mittens. Thankfully, my hands remained relaxed throughout the night, and I no longer harmed myself in my sleep.

Another problem solved.

It was frequently impossible for me to sleep through the night. I spent much of my time crying, dozing off and on, and worrying about the endless list of things I needed to either do or ask.

Again, with the lists...I began to keep a notepad and pen next to the bed. When I couldn't sleep, I wrote down my thoughts and the time. This often relieved my anxieties; I found comfort in the fact that I had made notes and wouldn't forget important things, and usually, I was able to go back to sleep.

Sometimes the notes proved to be very helpful. Other times, they read like gibberish. Regardless, by writing them down, I'd accomplished a task. I had compartmentalized my worries and traded them for a few hours of rest.

Along the way, I also discovered what not to do when trying to knock out the pain in my life.

The first has to do with alcohol.

This is true: I never had an alcoholic drink until I was in my mid-thirties, and then it was a glass of champagne at a wedding. However, a colleague who was aware of my new situation suggested that I drink a glass of wine before going to bed, to relax and become sleepy.

It worked the first couple of times, but soon, more was needed to lull me to sleep. Slowly, I increased the amount of wine I drank before going to bed.

I began to look forward to the end of the day and having wine. I really enjoyed the ritual of pouring the wine into the lovely goblet and sipping it throughout the evening. I liked the way it looked in my knock-off of a Waterford crystal goblet. I liked the smell of the deep red wine and the way it tasted sweeter after a few sips.

I felt my worries slip further away with each refill.

It wasn't long before my kids referred to the ever-present jug of Burgundy as "Mama's Liquid Crack." I laughed it off each night and played along with the joke. My friend had been right, and at last, I'd found a way to relax—that is until the night my kids witnessed me far too at ease.

Yet again, I'd fallen asleep on the sofa, empty goblet in hand. As was becoming the new routine, the kids woke me up before they went off to their own beds. However, this time, while attempting to get up, I rolled off the sofa and landed on the floor next to the cocktail table. I needed their help to get back on my feet, and I couldn't manage the walk to my bedroom on my own.

Not for the first time, I was clearly drunk.

As they put me to bed, I was slightly amused by the situation. However, I felt quite differently by the morning. With a clearer head, I was completely mortified by my prior behavior and lack of self-control. Most upsetting was that my children saw me in such a state.

I was more than bruised; I was disgusted and realized my new habit wasn't helping me in any way. In fact, it was hurting me in several ways. I still slept fitfully, but now I was also groggy in the morning, while none of my problems or worries were resolved. Additionally, I was increasingly spending money on my new habit that was needed for other things.

Most importantly, I realized this drunk wasn't the real me. It was an imposter, and I didn't like her.

That was a turning point. I quit drinking.

I emptied the remaining jug of wine and didn't buy another one. It wasn't easy; I missed it at first. But then, I thought of it as a new habit that could be changed like any other habit. I counted the days I went without a drink. Then, I counted the weeks that I didn't buy a jug of Burgundy. I replaced the ritual of pouring wine into a lovely goblet, with serving myself a juice or soda in the same goblet. And, as I always tend to do, I tracked these accomplishments on a list.

At ninety-one days, I knew that "Mama's Liquid Crack" was no longer a part of my life.

> *Don't be deceived by the pretty glass*
> *of red wine or its sweet aroma.*
> *It's tempting to think of it as a reward |*
> *or an escape, but in truth, it bites like a serpent,*
> *and stings like an adder.* Proverbs 23:31-32

The second attempt to dull my pain involved pre-scribed medication.

Several people suggested that I consider antidepres-sants, sedatives, or other medications to help me cope with the tough times. I had never considered these op-tions as something I wanted or needed.

However, during one of EJ's doctor's appointments, the physician's attention suddenly shifted to me. As I re-call, the doctor asked me a few questions about my sleep, my work, family matters and, lastly, she asked what made me happy. I remember being so deadened by the weight of my worries that I went blank and struggled to think of an answer. After an excruciatingly long pause, I respond-ed that I couldn't think of anything that made me happy.

I walked out of that meeting with an unsolicited pre-scription for an antidepressant. Although reluctant to acknowledge I had a problem, I also knew my family, colleagues and my work were suffering because of me. I decided to at least try something new, to make a change for the better.

It didn't really work out that way for me.

Yes, the destructive, constant worrying voices in my head became somewhat still. However, I also became less engaged in the world around me. So, while I appeared to be calmer and a much better listener, I was actually strug-gling to follow conversations or respond appropriately to situations.

Many times, I got it wrong.

It took a while for me to recognize that I had once again developed a harmful habit in an attempt to avoid pain. My choice was to stop the meds and work through the pain. This was very difficult at first and involved a lot of tears, temptations, self-doubt, and prayers.

Eventually, however, my path did include more joy than sorrow. And our days were filled with laughter and love once again.

If you need to reconsider your own choices, you will find what works best for you. I can only share my own experience; prayer and trust in God works better than alcohol and drugs.

I'm a "List Person," but now my lists grew longer and longer, and soon I was overwhelmed with the myriad details of my new life. Each day began with a review of the list I needed to complete. These included tasks related to EJ's medical care and benefits processing, communica-tions with the different facilities and staff, items needed to keep the household running, pay bills, fulfill family, and work responsibilities, and communicate with a large network of family and friends. There was zero time or desire for social interaction, nor was there a moment of downtime or rest for me.

Until I reached a breaking point, I hadn't realized that I had failed to include any items of self-care on these exhaustive agendas.

Life became a little more bearable once I began to compartmentalize my daily list, to include at least one item each providing for my spiritual, mental, and physical well-being. Even if that item was something at the most basic level of self-care, it made the list.

At first, the items were as simple as sitting quietly and enjoying one of my favorite things, a cup of chamomile tea. Eventually, the list expanded to include more items that provided me with a little comfort. These were actually quite simple and had the intended effect of lightening my heart.

I found comfort in watching classic TV comedies. Their familiarity and predictability sustained me as I felt connected to a collective, happier time. Never again would I take for granted the immense healing power of laughing out loud at an old episode of *I Love Lucy*. Perhaps you could start with viewing the episodes where Lucy is filming an energy tonic commercial or gets into a tussle while stomping grapes in Italy; they still work every time for me.

I highly recommend picking and enjoying your own favorite classics, no matter how silly they may seem in today's busy, demanding world.

The following are some other practical, high-impact, cost-free, alcohol-free, drug-free prescriptive ideas for caregivers who truly need a break from their worries and demanding lives.

Pray Like Your Lives Depend Upon It

When you pray, enter your closet alone, and when
you have shut your door, pray to your Father in
secret; and your Father which sees in secret shall
reward you openly.
Matthew 6:6

It was my habit to do my household chores on Saturday mornings. On this particular day, it occurred to me that I hadn't seen EJ for a little while. I began to search the house while trying to tamp down my fears that I would find him collapsed on the floor or worse. The longer my search to find EJ continued, the more difficult it became to ignore my fears.

Eventually, I discovered a rustling noise coming from the guest room walk-in closet. I opened the door slowly, afraid that I was going to find some critter. Happily, instead of an unwelcomed visitor, I found my husband standing in front of the few odds and ends stored there. Amongst the items, was a beautiful painting of Jesus.

"Ah, there you are! I was starting to worry about you."

EJ seemed surprised at my relief at having found him safe, in his own home. When I asked him what he was doing, he responded, "Why, I'm in my closet to pray, of course."

"Oh, excuse me, Sweetheart. I didn't mean to interrupt you."

"That's okay. We're almost through," EJ responded.

I closed the door softly, sat down on the bed and waited for him to finish his prayers. I was so happy EJ was having this private time to commune with God. While waiting, I took advantage of the quiet time to pray myself;

I was very grateful for the time to reflect on the sweetness of life. After several minutes, EJ returned to the room and stated he was ready for some ice cream. And, of course, I made sure he got what he wanted, with a cherry on top.

Your spirit needs nourishment, too. Keep your Bible or other materials that provide you comfort, guidance and inspiration close at hand. Find your "closet" and pray for your loved ones, others, and yourself. Express your thankfulness for another day of life and love.

Feel God's protection and care for you.

Move. Breathe. Shake It All Out.

Take a break, take a walk, take deep breaths, stretch in place, or just stand up and move around the room. Turn up the music and dance like nobody's watching. Or, if you're like me and blessed with great rhythm, dance like everyone's watching.

Can't take the time or don't have the inclination to go to a gym? There are things you can do in the privacy of your own home at whatever level of physical activity you desire. Even a slow walk up and down the stairs or using small hand weights and walking in place have their benefits.

However small these bursts of activity may be, they can make a big difference in your health, perspective, and attitude.

Rest and Refresh Your Mind

Your mind needs a break, too.

Engaging in a new or different activity may bring you some respite from your worries, especially during the long quiet hours when sleep seems impossible. Try something that doesn't include screen time once in a while.

This may include books, sketch pad, journal, crosswords, or earbuds to listen to your music, podcasts, etc.

Turn off the television's relentless blue light and mindless programming. You can afford to miss another string of ads about "wonder products" and personal injury attorneys.

Accept the Help of Others

If you're fortunate enough to have someone ask you, "What can we do to help?" or "Is there anything you need?" overcome the usual response of "Thank you, we're fine." Instead, accept their offers and give them a few suggestions of the things you would consider helpful. Most people are very happy to be given some guidance on the things you would really appreciate and would make your family's life easier. Let them pick up supplies for you, run errands, bring you something, take messages, return calls, etc.

No matter how self-reliant and strong you think you are, now is the time to let them help you. Focus on what really matters (YOU and your loved one!), not a never-ending list of things to keep you up at night.

Somehow, it's true that the important stuff always gets accomplished anyway.

Other Suggestions that Worked for Me:

- Take a nap, a bath, or a shower.
- Write, tackle a jigsaw puzzle (I loved doing them online! I could pick them up and pause them, anytime and anywhere), download a new game app.
- Cozy up with a pet.

- Take it one day at a time.

- Go outside, sit in the sun, listen to the birds. Set a timer for at least five minutes.

- Slow down, feel your body relax and your tension melt away.

- Speak with a spiritual counselor, a mental health counselor, or someone else that you trust and is well qualified to help you.

- Join a support group or find a way to connect with other groups with similar interests.

- Talk with someone you care for and who cares for you too. Take the time to catch up on what's going on in their lives. It was nice to feel "normal" again while sharing conversations that included my friends' activities and news, rather than being so self-absorbed with all the issues happening in in our home.

Isolation and Loneliness

It's very common for there to be an initial rush of concern and support from others following a critical event. However, all but a few truly close friends and loved ones can or are willing to sustain that level of care over an extended time. It's understandable, but the result is that as your need for help may actually deepen over time, the level of support you receive is probably slowly diminishing.

It's during these most difficult times that it is so very easy for caregivers to gradually lose connections with friends and family, resulting in deep feelings of isolation and loneliness. These feelings can be overwhelming for the caregiver, leaving them with the belief that this is the natural consequence of events and, whether they like it or not, also their fate in life.

I was slow to recognize the progression of EJ's dementia and even slower to see its impact on me. Over time I'd begun to generally understand a variety of trigger points that caused him anxiety, fear, frustration, and anger. He seemed especially vulnerable in crowds and fearful during medical visits, became exasperated easily and lost his temper over the smallest of disappointments.

These behaviors were the direct opposite of my husband's true nature. Yet, these were very real behaviors in the moment, and we had to manage through them.

He developed the impulsivity of a child yet had the size and strength of a grown man, which made it challenging to dissuade him from behaving or speaking inappropriately. Attending social gatherings, going to restaurants, and running errands that would have previously been considered routine activities became very difficult to navigate. Whenever possible, I declined to participate in team-building activities outside of normal work hours, especially if spouses were included.

I could no longer foresee with certainty how EJ would react to a situation. Aside from his emotional reactions, it also became a struggle to constrain him on a more frequent basis, as he increasingly approached strangers and their children as they shopped. Other diners in restaurants found it very confusing and intrusive when he wanted to strike up a conversation with them or join them at their tables. Sometimes, I was able to intercede or diffuse the situation, but I wasn't always successful.

Although EJ's intentions were good, and he just wanted to talk, understandably, not everyone welcomed his approach. Generally, after a few moments of interaction with him, people understood EJ's condition and moved on. However, more than once, a protective father threatened to harm EJ, as did the man who appeared to be Middle Eastern, in response to being greeted as Bin Laden by my husband. I was able to intervene but only just in time.

I was frightened for my husband, sad for him and exhausted.

Once I could no longer predict or control my husband's actions, I realized it was no longer safe for him to interact with strangers or be in unfamiliar places. Frankly, everywhere, including home, was becoming more unfamiliar to him by the day. For these reasons, I began to withdraw from all but the most necessary contact with others and our closest friends.

As a result, we both became more removed from interactions with others, even those we loved.

Whether because of fatigue, time demands or EJ's current state of health and mind, I began turning down invitations to social events we would have enjoyed earlier. Instead, we stayed home together.

Piece by piece, I distanced myself from friends and became more isolated. I saw no way out, even as I felt the crushing weight of loneliness on my heart.

However, we were blessed to have a few friends and family members who never gave up on us. They never stopped reaching out and continued to invite us to holiday dinners and small outings. On the rare occasions when we ventured out, they did everything they could to ensure EJ's comfort and assist me with his care. These friends never took offense at having their invitations turned down. Instead, they offered words of encouragement and ended the conversation with, "You're not off the hook yet, my friend. Promise me you'll join us the next time."

If only on a temporary basis, my spirits were lifted at the thought that we were not forgotten by our friends; they were not letting us slip away quite so easily.

Encouragement, Resilience and Healing

We all need spiritual nourishment, just as the flowers in the garden need watering. Those who have the responsibility of caring for others especially need their energy, confidence and joy replenished on a regular basis.

I certainly needed this more frequently than I ever let others know.

Reading, quiet reflection, and prayer were the most effective ways for me to get back on track, find inspiration and gain a renewed belief in life; they still are.

You'll find your own way to best accomplish the rejuvenation you need, or perhaps you already have.

For me, the following citations and quotes share the common threads of imparting hope, encouragement, and protection from harm. Each time I revisited them, I felt as if I'd just experienced a soft summer rain and was now slowly stretching to greet the sun's first warming embrace.

I was left feeling safe and loved; and that's a very good thing.

Be still, listen, and know that I am your God, always.
Psalm 46:10

Stand therefore, in truth, and having on the breastplate of righteousness. Ephesians 6:14

What does the Lord require of me, but to do justly, and to love mercy, and to walk humbly with my God? Micah 6:8

When I am afraid, I will trust in God. Psalm 56:3

Daughter, take heart: your faith has made you whole. And immediately, the woman was healed. Matthew 9:22

I have heard your prayer, I have seen your tears, and I will heal you. 2 Kings 20:5

Come unto me, all that labor and are heavy laden, and I will give you rest. Matthew 11:28

Who loves you, Baby?! - Mom

The past is gone, the future is not here, now I am free of both. Right now, I choose joy. - Deepak Chopra

A depressing and difficult passage has prefaced every page I have turned in life. - Charlotte Bronte

Although the world is full of suffering, it is also full of the overcoming of it. - Helen Keller

Remember, no one can make you feel inferior without your consent. - Eleanor Roosevelt

You'll be bothered from time to time by storms, fog, and snow. When you are, think of those who went through it before you, and say to yourself, 'What they could do, I can do.' - Antoine de Saint-Exupéry

I will trust in the Lord with all my heart; and rely on him, not simply my own understanding. Proverbs 3:5-6

Even when I am overwhelmed and my spirit seems broken, God already knows my path and will save me. Psalm 142:3

I will lead you through these trials; you will not stumble. Jeremiah 31:9

For you are my rock and my fortress; therefore, I know you will lead me and guide me. Psalm 31:3

I will instruct you and teach you in the way which you are to go, I will guide you. Psalm 32:8

Weeping may last for a night, but joy comes in the morning. Psalm 30:5

I will give all my worries to God; for he cares for me. I can do no better than this. 1Peter 5:7

He will be very gracious to me when I cry; he will hear it and he will answer me. My job is to listen for his voice and follow his instruction. Isaiah 30:19

Each of us must find our own source of strength, no matter how temporary it may seem at the time. Much like the Chinese philosopher Lao Tzu said, "A journey of a thousand miles begins with one step." And so, begins the journey of taking care of yourself.

You will find the healing nourishment you need for your heart, your mind, and your body, one small smile and one step at a time.

STEPPINGSTONES

ɔ I must maintain the critical balance between spiritual, physical, and mental wellness. I can do this one step at a time.

ɔ In whatever way I try, attempting to numb my feelings doesn't work for me. I must seek to understand, learn, and grow. It can be very painful, but must not be avoided. In the end, it never is.

ɔ It's not selfish to follow my own advice to others about self-care. It's the oxygen needed to keep me going. Start by shutting out feelings of inadequacy, fear, and anger. Build on those quiet, valuable, life-affirming times.

ɔ When others want to help, don't be shy about letting them know *how* they can help.

ɔ My soul, my spirit, my mind, and my heart need nourishment at all times. Some days more is required than on others. Yet, I'm not afraid of doing this work, for I am not alone.

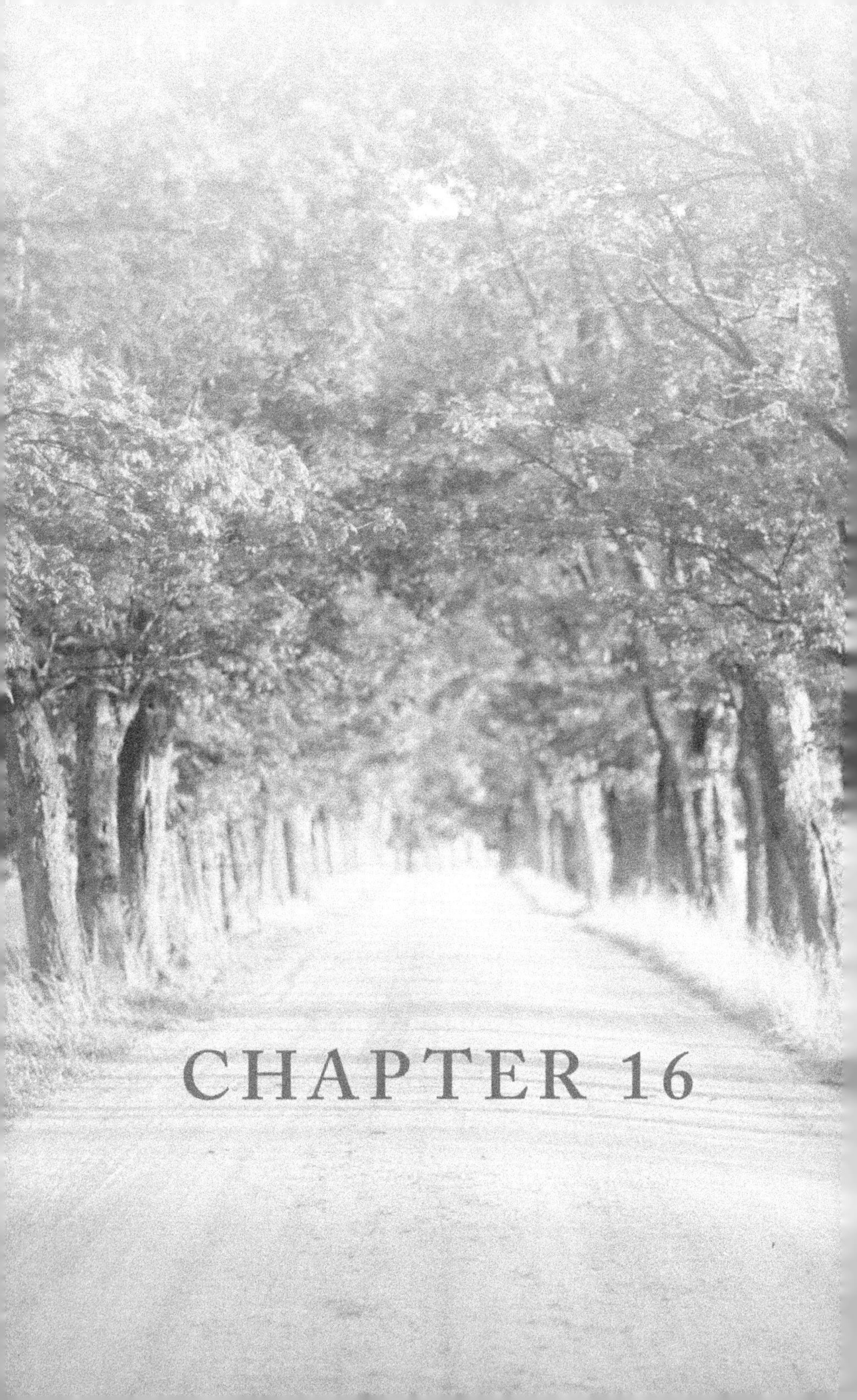

CHAPTER 16

Alarm Bells

The LORD doesn't see us as man sees us; for man
looks on our outward appearance,
but God looks on our heart.
1 Samuel 16:7

"When wealth is lost, nothing is lost;
when health is lost, something is lost;
when character is lost, all is lost."
- Billy Graham

There are some opening lines and comments from others that instantly set off alarm bells for me.

Depending upon our prior relationship or the context of the conversation, these alarms may be downgraded to a yellow warning or, conversely, upgraded to a red alarm. Eventually, I learned to trust my instincts and measure my responses accordingly.

This approach was put to the test on a regular basis during my years as a caregiver.

"I'm only saying this for your own good."

RED ALERT!

Unless you are my parent, a doctor, my spiritual advisor, or a trusted friend, then no, you are not saying this for my own good.

You don't know me, my family, or my life.

What you are saying is for your own good or you simply believe that you are all-knowing. In the first instance, shame on you; in the second case, I think we can all agree there is only One All-Knowing, and it's not you.

Now that response might seem a little harsh, but it is born from experience.

A few weeks into EJ's hospital internment, I received a very disturbing call from some person with the insurance company. She went through the details of the benefit plan, using terms and acronyms I barely understood. Before she ended the call, she stated that she wanted to address a sensitive issue with me.

"I'm only saying this for your own good," she stated, and without pausing for a response from me, she launched into a cold dialogue, informing me that based upon my husband's condition, my life, as I knew it, was over. Further, she proclaimed my husband's life, if he survived the next few weeks, would never be the same.

She forecasted that he would probably remain in a vegetative state or, at best, recover to the level of a two-year-old. She cautioned me to be prepared that he would not know me or other family members. As I remained in stunned silence, she gave me the direction that, "It's time for you to move on." And said, yet again, "I'm only saying this for your own good."

I was left speechless.

Thankfully, she was completely wrong then and proved to be wrong throughout the ensuing twenty-plus years of my life with my husband.

Initially, I wondered how a stranger could attempt to insert herself into my life without the authority to do so. What could be the motivation for such a cold, heartless and wrong dialogue?

Sadly, that wasn't the only time someone, whether known to me or a stranger, said hateful or hurtful things to me, under the cloak of concern for my welfare. Those conversations frequently started with, "I'm only saying this for your own good."

"No offense, but . . ."

RED ALERT!

I don't know, perhaps we all react to this opening line the same way or it may just be a peculiarity of mine. However, anytime the other person thinks they're about to offend me, I'm already on the alert that I will be or should be offended.

The speaker has let me know they are about to ask a question or make a comment that is too personal and just flat out none of their business.

Unfortunately, many people—including otherwise dear friends—can be curious or have opinions about things that shouldn't concern them. Somehow, my husband's medical event seemed to open the doors for these kinds of intrusive conversations.

My reaction was entirely dependent upon the regard and affection I had for the speaker. Depending upon that status, the response might be a deadly silence or a laughing, "I'm already offended; don't go any farther. Let's talk about something else."

With others, I used a very effective method to shut down a conversation that began with the dreaded, "No offense but..."

"Hey, don't worry about it, but first, I have a list of probably offensive questions I've been wanting to ask you. Let me go first, this time," I quickly interrupted the speaker and asked earnestly.

Needless to say, no one ever agreed to that deal and the conversations went no further.

I should be ashamed of my rudeness toward them, I guess. But I'm not. I have no regrets for cutting off people who are willing to hurt me or mine and place their own interests over our welfare. My advice: don't think twice about deflecting hurtful people; you get to choose whether to engage with them.

I think of it this way, nobody can treat you like a doormat, unless you first lay down.

"He would have wanted this . . ."

RED ALERT!

It's amazing how many people claim to possess a clairvoyant ability to know what someone else is thinking or would have wanted.

This phrase is most often used to manipulate you into a decision that provides the other person with *their* desired outcome. Although their motive may be well-intentioned—and I'm being generous here—they are nonetheless attempting to influence you by claiming to know what your loved one would want.

Regardless of family or friendship affiliations, no one knows your loved one better than you. And if you don't know exactly what to do, and you've asked the relevant professionals for advice, just trust your heart, trust your gut, and make the best decision you are able.

Disgustingly, "He would have wanted this . . ." was used by men repeatedly, when explaining they wanted to sleep with me. Of course, they presented this as an act of kindness, something to help ease my sadness and find a way out of my loneliness.

I was shocked by this approach used by my friend, my husband's friend, our neighbor, a co-worker, and a few others. More than once, I was also told by an offending man that it was okay with his wife and all right if I thought of my husband while we made love.

They made my stomach turn.

I'll keep my responses private, but suffice it to say, no one ever brought it up twice.

"I've always wanted to ask you . . ."

Yellow Alert on this one.

What changed? Why are you asking me now? I immediately wondered upon hearing this statement. Again, somehow, it was as if my husband's illness made it okay to ask very personal questions that would have never been broached before.

This was especially true in the first weeks following EJ's stroke. Men in particular asked me very personal questions about EJ's prior health, family history and personal wellness habits. I quickly understood they were searching for an answer that would exclude themselves from a similar fate. They found no comfort in the answers to their questions; EJ was healthy, watched his diet, exercised regularly and had no family history of strokes.

Soon, I became aware that people think they can ask or tell a caregiver anything. Sometimes they're motivated by love and concern. Sadly, I also learned, oftentimes, they're motivated by selfish or perverse interests.

No additional examples of the multiple intrusive questions I received are needed here. You'll undoubtedly have several from your own experiences.

Please, learn quickly not to be shocked or hurt by those who have crossed a line.

Most of the time, they will have simply made a stupid, thoughtless mistake, based upon their overactive curiosity. In these situations, let the person know that you don't choose to answer the question. It's okay to add, "And please don't ask me that again."

Anyone who cares about you should understand your response and may even be embarrassed or regretful about their comments. This person will know you don't intend to be rude; you've just spoken your truth.

Others may react as if you have misunderstood or offended them. In these situations, it's helpful to remember offenders and liars often like to flip the script and play the victim . . . because it usually works.

Be careful not to get caught up in trying to make them feel better. After all, they chose their words and actions deliberately. Just respond with a simple, "No worries, let's talk about something else," and move on.

You really do have more important things to think about.

When it's more than that, perhaps even malicious, consider carefully and choose wisely those you allow to stay close to you and your family. You don't need anyone in your circle who doesn't have the best intentions toward you.

It may, in fact, be time to prune your list of "friends."

"I deserve this."

Yellow Alert

Hmmmm . . . Well, maybe I do or maybe I don't deserve the treat I'm contemplating.

A caregiver's life isn't tolerable if it only includes self-sacrifice or complete denial of the things and activities that, at least in some small way, make us happy. Yet, invoking this phrase usually meant I was trying to manage negotiations between my inner parent and child, my self-control versus my indulgent self.

I already knew I was trying to justify doing something that wasn't in my long-term best interests.

Consider, are you about to reward yourself for a goal you've accomplished or are you perhaps celebrating a victory? Is the reward in balance with the achievement and will this be something you will enjoy? Will it bring you happiness?

If so, go for it!

However, I most often tried to rationalize any unhealthy, frivolous, or too expensive decisions by employing the argument "I deserve this." This phrase popped into my mind frequently, and I used it to justify many things including another glass of wine, a piece of jewelry or other purchases I couldn't really afford and designer shoes for a life I didn't actually lead. I still blame the shoes on watching too many episodes of *Sex and the City*.

Bad choices all, and I knew better!

"I deserve this" is a victim's mentality and never served me well.

"You're a saint; I don't know how you do it."

Yellow Alert

These words were greatly comforting to me—the first time I heard them.

The kind and gentle speaker was expressing her concern and admiration for me. It felt good; made me feel a little less lost in the swirling tornado that had sucked up our lives. Her words made me feel like someone else recognized this wasn't fair, and it was HARD work for me to just get through each day.

It was a little seductive to think of myself as a saint, especially during difficult times. However, I slowly became aware of the hidden dangers of believing this phrase.

It was a lie; I wasn't a saint.

My husband and I were partners. I didn't rank above him; I wasn't greater than him or, for that matter, anyone else. Since I wasn't a victim, there was no need to focus on the "fairness of life" and whether I "deserved" this.

I was simply a woman whose husband got sick.

I had the same flaws after I became a caregiver that I did before his critical medical event. I was still impatient and a bit of a smart-ass. Those who knew me best could easily expand upon my long, personal, "Needs Improvement" list.

However, as a caregiver, my self-indulgent ways now had to become secondary to the efforts required to care for my husband and children. As a deeply loved and formerly indulged princess, I didn't know how to accomplish this transition, but I improved simply through trial and error.

This is way above my paygrade. I can't do this anymore, I often thought. I wanted to give up, go to sleep forever, have this pain stop. And then I'd think about the people I loved and those who loved me.

The morning always came, and I knew I had to find the energy to fulfill my responsibilities and grind it out again that day. My family needed me, and I needed them.

No, I wasn't a saint; I was quite simply a wife and a mother.

"No one could blame you . . ."

RED ALERT!

"You're only forty-four and still a young woman with needs of your own. No one could blame you for taking some nice man as a lover."

My sweet friend thought she was being compassionate by suggesting that it was time for me to have a relationship with someone outside of my marriage. She was aware of my husband's condition, the changes in our relationship and what my life as a caregiver involved.

I know deep in my heart that she wanted nothing but the best for me.

Yet, she seemed surprised when I answered, "I'm a married woman. I love my husband, and he's still my husband. Please don't bring that up again."

With a sad nod, she turned away from me. We never spoke of it again.

"Till death do us part" was more than a promise made on a beautiful day. It was a tattoo on my heart. Sometimes it was a very real and painful struggle just to make it through the next hour, the next night, the next day. I could only rely on love to guide me through this trial.

My decision to remain faithful was because I deeply loved my husband, and he loved me. That didn't change because of his stroke.

I have no judgment about the choices of others. However, I know who I am, and more importantly, I know who I am not.

Those two things don't vary because of a change in my, or our, circumstances.

STEPPINGSTONES

∽ Stay alert. Watch out for the snakes in the garden.

∽ Set boundaries with others whenever necessary.

∽ No matter the circumstances, stay true to myself, true to my values.

∽ I've come to believe that 98 percent of people are caring and helpful. As for the other 2 percent, well, may God show them how to change their hearts. In the meantime, I won't let them distract me or skew my perception of what's right.

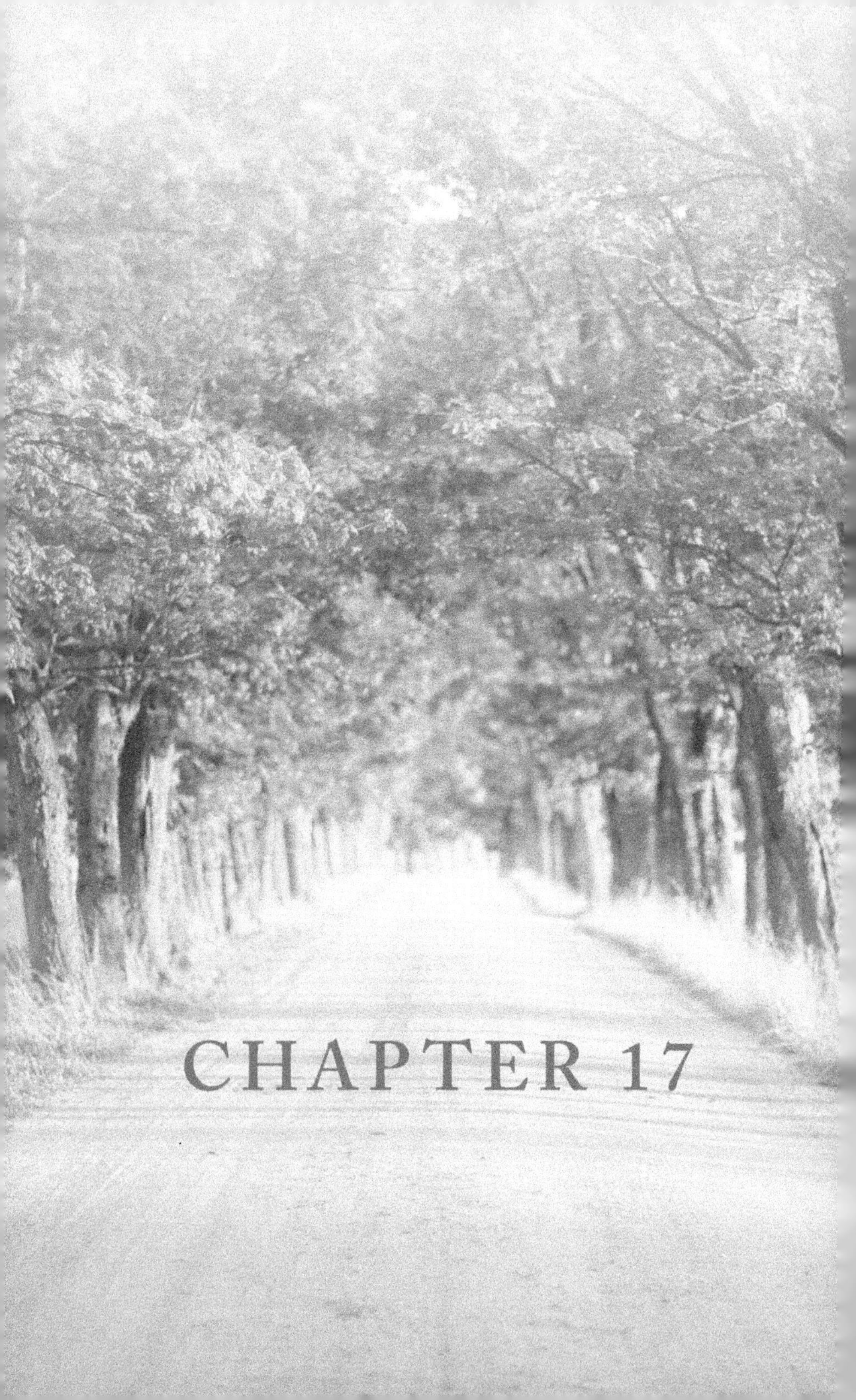

CHAPTER 17

Embrace the New Normal

What is essential is invisible to the eye.
- Antoine de Saint-Exupéry

*The greatest happiness in life is the conviction
that we are loved; loved for ourselves, or rather,
loved in spite of ourselves.*
- Victor Hugo

*Where your pleasure is, there is your treasure:
where your treasure, there your heart;
where your heart, there your happiness.*
- St. Augustine

*Regardless of our changing circumstances,
I am my beloved's, and my beloved is mine.*
Song of Solomon 6:3

I came to understand that our new normal meant that noth-ing was *normal*. Everything could and did often change in the blink of an eye. I abandoned the expectation that any-thing would be routine or "normal" ever again.

Surprisingly, there was great freedom in this change of mindset.

At some point, I transitioned from experiencing continuing grief and longing for "the old days" to accepting and embracing the current multitude of blessings in our lives. At the same time, I began to experience more joy than pain, on a daily basis. When I did encounter disappointments or challenges, I tried to remember the words of one of my forever favorite literary heroes, The Little Prince.

I need to put up with a few caterpillars
if I want to get to know the butterflies.
- Antoine de Saint-Exupéry

EJ's physical circumstances hadn't really improved, in fact, he was declining in several areas. He still was partially paralyzed and increasingly struggled with the onset of both Parkinson's and dementia. Additionally, he began to fall more frequently and suffered many other physical challenges on a more frequent basis.

During this time, a dear friend asked me if my love for him had changed since I no longer had the husband that I had before.

"I still have my husband; I just like to think of him as a younger version of himself. You see, EJ explained to me that, after the stroke, he felt like he was born again (in a physical sense, not in a spiritual one). He had to learn to sit up, walk, talk and everything else, all over again. Progress has taken years, but he now thinks of himself as thirteen years old. But, whenever EJ brings that up, I ask him, 'Well, what man isn't?'" My friend laughed and nodded in agreement before I continued.

"And I love that thirteen-year-old. I don't think of him as a patient or a burden. I'm honored to be his wife."

It was true that through it all, our love had deepened; we just expressed it differently than in the past. Although our life had serious challenges, it was also filled with newfound happiness and impromptu laughter.

In the best sense, our world slowed down, became smaller and much more intimate. It was now just the two of us, in our own little world. Our time together became filled with observations about the smallest of things, the beauty of life and the joy of our shared experiences.

Dementia certainly changed the way my husband viewed the world and navigated it. Consequently, my experience also was greatly enhanced by the new way he decoded the universe and shared his understanding of a more beautiful, gentler, joyous existence, filled with love for all.

This formerly reserved (around all but family and close friends), sometimes terse "man of science" was now easily moved to tears by the splendor of this world. It was a privilege to share that world with him.

One Saturday while on our monthly trip to Costco, my husband was staring out of the passenger seat window and listening to some "oldie" music on the radio. Slowly he turned to me; his eyes brimming with tears. Silently, he began to cry, and I felt a sharp clutch at my heart as his tears spilled over, leaving small tracks down his face.

"Honey, what's wrong? Are you okay? Do I need to pull over?" I quickly checked to see if I could safely navigate our red Ford Explorer to the shoulder of the road.

"I'm okay. I'm fine. It's just so beautiful; everything's so beautiful. You, here, now, the music. . .. It's just so beautiful. I'm the luckiest man on earth. No matter what happens, this is heaven now."

I'll never forget his sweet smile as he wiped his tears away, shook his head and laughed oh so quietly while we continued on our way. I don't know if he noticed as I wiped away my own tears. It didn't really matter; we were both content and felt blessed to have each other in our lives.

In those few shared, intimate moments, we'd experienced heaven indeed. It was a blessing to be by his side, however long it might last.

* * *

July 4, 2012
    EJ: "Honey, what day is today?"
    Me: "It's the fourth of July."
    EJ: "Great! I've been wanting some birthday cake!"

Of course, I hurriedly made a cake to celebrate our country's official birthdate. EJ was happy and I was grateful for another joy-filled day with him.

* * *

Late one evening while I was in my home office working on a presentation due the next morning, EJ plopped into the big chair next to my desk. He seemed not to notice I was completely absorbed in completing my tasks.

"Honey, have I ever told you how the French saved the world?" he asked me. Having been born in Dijon, France, his script had a slightly one-sided version of the greatness of the French.

Throughout the years I'd listen repeatedly as he struggled to retell an old story, and I always pretended to hear it for the first time. This story, starting with the ancient warrior Vercingetorix in 82 BC through the medical contributions of the Curies, was an all-time favorite of his and had been retold on a regular basis over the past several years.

However, on this particular night, I had a lot of work to be completed before bedtime. So, I told the truth.

"Yes, My Love, you have told me that story before."

"Many times?"

"Yes, Sweetheart, many, many times."

"Good! I'm really tired tonight. It's your turn to tell it to me this time." He slapped his knee and laughed so hard at his own joke that his eyes watered, and his shoulders shook.

EJ was clearly very pleased with himself for springing such an exquisite trap on me.

"I love you, Sucker, but it's a sad state of affairs when you start asking me to tell *your* stories to myself!" We both belly laughed, while wiping the tears from our eyes.

* * *

Sleep was hard to come by and I didn't appreciate being awakened at three in the morning by lively piano music. Well, to be fair, it's quite a stretch to call it music; it was a sort of rapid, chaotic banging of the keys in search of a tune. I tried to gather my thoughts, as I headed up the stairs to see what was going on.

I discovered EJ and Ajax sitting side by side on the piano bench. Each froze silently in place and, with widened eyes, stared straight at me. Ajax's paws remained still on the piano keys next to EJ's hands. They both looked guilty as if having been caught in the act of committing some great crime.

"Now you've spoiled our surprise for you. We were writing a love song," EJ said with a crooked smile.

"Sorry for the interruption, Ajax. Let's try to finish it later," he apologized, as the cat jumped down from the bench and trotted away. Mid-retreat, Ajax paused just long enough to glance backward at me with a narrow-eyed dismissal. Clearly, I had spoiled his early morning fun.

Once back in bed, EJ fell asleep straight away. I, however, was kept awake chuckling at the memory of my two guys caught in the collaborative act of composing the best tribute to love ever.

Sometimes, when the Florida mosquitos weren't too bad, we rocked on the front porch, watching for animal shapes in the clouds and comparing our thoughts on the weather. We'd count the stars and connect the celestial dots to make up images and tell each other tall tales about their meanings. Other times, when hearing a Cole Porter song or other familiar classic tune, we'd join in, purposefully and loudly warbling out of tune together.

Our outlandish and screeching discord made us laugh out loud. We gave no thought that our neighbors might not enjoy the serenade, although the pets gave very clear indications of their displeasure.

Moondoggy usually got up and moved further away from us, as if to avoid our voices. Ajax watched our shenanigans with a narrowly slanted critical eye, while perched on the porch swing. Neither chose to join in the singing.

* * *

Never missing the opportunity to wave at the neighbors passing by our front porch, EJ always called out to them *bonjour* or *bon nuit*. He toasted them with whatever was in his one functioning hand. This might be a cold beer, a Klondike bar, or some other object. It didn't matter; no passerby—no matter the age, friend, or stranger—escaped his greeting and salute.

It also became routine for him to attempt to carry on a conversation with them in French. Each time I reminded him that our friends didn't speak French, he responded, "Well, they should! How will they learn if nobody teaches them?" and continued as if they were engaged in a two-way conversation. Our neighbors would smile understandingly, wave goodbye and continue their walks.

* * *

One glorious Spring evening, we were at our usual stations, rocking on the front porch with Moondoggy and Ajax nearby at their customary stations. We were perfectly content to gaze at the approaching sunset together in silence.

"It's hard to believe that today's our seventy-sixth wedding anniversary. I should have bought you something; we should have had a party," EJ said, while never missing a beat of the rhythmic rocking of his chair. I rather liked the soft squeaking of the white wooden chair against the charcoal grey painted porch top.

"Sweetheart, that would make me well over one hundred years old." I laughed, in return. I intended to let him know it wasn't our anniversary, and we'd been married just fourteen years, but I didn't have the chance.

"Wow, girl! You're looking really good for your age." He was truly incredulous and shook his head in amazement. I let go of being offended or trying to figure out how old he believed I was and just smiled at the intended compliment.

"Is it too late for you to make us an anniversary cake?"

"Yes, but we still have some of those cookies I made the other day. And there's butter pecan ice cream. We can have those now and pretend they're cake if you'd like."

"Yay, cookies!" he said as we returned inside to start the faux-anniversary celebrations with Moondoggy and Ajax following closely behind us.

* * *

Although our lives were chaotic, unpredictable, and painful in so many ways, we made time to share these small joys together. Our relationship now included a different, yet deeper level of intimacy and our bond became even stronger than before.

Frequently and with open hearts, we spoke of our gratitude for the beauty of this world and its many examples of God's love.

Once in bed for the night, we held hands and said the *Lord's Prayer* together. EJ would lead, and although occasionally there might have been a stumble or two, he would always end with an emphatic and loud "Amen!"

It reminded me of our impatient kids, wanting to rush through our prayers of gratitude for the Lord's bounty and go straight to the Thanksgiving feast before them. With this vision in mind, I couldn't help but smile, as we said goodnight.

I had become accustomed to this "new normal" world, in which EJ so seamlessly slipped between his competing realities.

Increasingly, he dwelt on a small personal planet of happiness where since age had no relevance, grandchildren might easily be confused for their parents, pets spoke with him, and everyone he encountered wanted to speak French. Thankfully, no matter his condition, EJ never became confused about me; he knew who I was, and he continually let me know I was loved.

Although at any moment EJ might not recall where he lived, who was President of the United States or the correct year, it didn't really matter. I could take care of those small details of life. He was happy in his very real world that wasn't connected to the experiences of the rest of us. Eventually, I became less fearful of his confusions and learned to simply appreciate that we were able to share another day.

At other times, EJ was acutely aware of his losses and limitations. These fleeting moments were terrifying, deeply saddening, and frustrating for him. However difficult these interludes were for both of us, I never let him know that I was hurting for him, hurting for us. I hoarded these feelings until I was alone.

Once in solitude, I wept until there were no tears left to water the earth.

STEPPINGSTONES

- Everything is changing. It's often a bit scary, but there's also a new freedom that comes with accepting this truth.

- Our small, lovely world brings the most joy to me.

- What a blessing it is to have someone to dream with, to laugh with, to know so well and to care about, oh so very well.

- To love and to know that I am loved, is the greatest blessing of all.

CHAPTER 18

Angel Encounters

Be kind to strangers: for you may be
entertaining angels without knowing it.
Hebrews 13:2

"Angels are pure thoughts from God,
winged with Truth and Love."
- Mary Baker Eddy

The angels of the Lord surround those that love
and obey him and the angels will protect them.
Psalm 34:7

For he shall give his angels charge over you,
to keep you in all your ways.
Psalm 91:11

This I know: there are angels amongst us.

I understand angels to be messages from God, and they come when we need them the most. These messages open and expand our thought to the unseen possibilities that already surround us.

You will know angels by the clarity, comfort, guidance, and joy they bring. Whatever form these messengers take, you will know it's a real encounter and feel their guiding, healing presence. You will feel their touch in your heart. The messages these angels impart are the true "disruptors" in our lives. An encounter with them can change your heart and mind in a moment.

Listen for them, trust them, and let them in.

It was another especially difficult day and I was visiting my husband who had recently been readmitted to the hospital. I was discouraged about his status, as I had not yet received any information about a possible date for his return home. As I made my way to his room, my thoughts were cluttered with another of my very long "to do" lists including insurance issues, work responsibilities and family matters. All were equally important and demanding more time than I actually had to give.

*I don't know how to do all of this. I'm overwhelmed and feel like a total failure. I don't like this feeling; no, I really **hate** feeling like this. I'm so tired.* This familiar refrain played through my mind.

Relief from the weight of these burdensome thoughts had become a very rare experience for me.

Suddenly, the lovely sound of a small gospel chorus singing in one of the rooms further down the corridor interrupted my chaotic, internal dialogue. They were evidently visiting a very fortunate patient. Although the songs were unfamiliar to me, their hymns were beautiful, their harmonies heavenly and the glorious music uplifted my heart as I continued down the long hallway. I didn't know the location of their joyful performance but thought how fortunate we all were to receive such a gift.

However, all too soon, the singing stopped.

How sad, I was really enjoying that. I'd like to hear more of their music, I lamented.

As I entered my husband's room, to my great surprise, I discovered the group was actually with EJ. The six men were now standing, holding hands, and loudly praying over his bedside. Although he appeared to be unconscious and was a stranger to them, they prayed fervently for his healing. I stood still, bowed my head, silently listened to their powerful words, and joined them in those moments of communion with God. I'm sure EJ was aware of their prayers and benefited from this unsolicited offering of pure love.

I know I did.

As I thanked the group, I was moved to tears by their grace and generosity. Their warm smiles and farewell blessings shot straight to my heart. I felt the presence of angels and received their healing message. My distracted thoughts were cleared and I was able to focus on a loving and joyful visit with my husband. I felt renewed hope and gratitude for God's care for us.

What can be greater than that?

Unfortunately, I wasn't able to sustain my joy at having encountered the gospel group for long after EJ's release from the care facility.

Within a few months, EJ was in the hospital, again. Another fall, another seizure, and mental confusion had taken their tolls. He needed more care than I could provide at home. The only available space for him was at a facility with marginal Florida State ratings. Our VA representative assured me that he would be moved as soon as a space became available at a different facility.

I was fed up with our life and generally angry at everyone.

Although in my heart I knew it was wrong, I resented those who were happy, hated the doctors who couldn't make my husband better and thought about "divorcing" family members who offered no help yet, gave almost as much unfounded advice as they did criticism of my efforts. Clueless about the cost of EJ's care, medical expenses, available facilities, and the VA benefits process these family members let it be known that they questioned my decisions. Not so subtly, they also questioned our financial status and wondered out loud how EJ's money was being managed.

It was early in the morning, yet I was already agitated with the world and decided to go for a short walk before getting ready for yet another trip to the hospital.

As I walked, I chewed over my long list of grievances. Nothing and no one were spared, not even the unknown drivers who were whizzing by me. From time to time, I found myself angrily talking out loud to my imagined army of adversaries. As I worked my way down my mental Enemies List, I was brutal, won every conjured-up skirmish and relished each imagined victory.

Evidently unaware of who it was messing with, a small bird kept coming at me from behind. It was impossible to ignore as it followed me for several blocks. Although it didn't hit me, the bird was flying far too close for my comfort. Repeatedly, I tried to wave it away, but couldn't shake it.

I was greatly annoyed.

Understandably, the winged aggressor got added to my Enemies List and landed in one of the Top Five spots.

All at once, the bird changed tactics; it dive-bombed me. This time, it grabbed a few strands of my hair. Startled, furious and now ready to do battle, I looked up to see a stunning, scarlet-colored bird that had been trying to get my attention.

How had I missed that?

I had been so preoccupied with anger and staring at the ground before me, that I never bothered to look up. I almost missed an encounter with one of my favorite beings in the world, a cardinal.

I've always felt comforted by the presence or images of a cardinal. While there are many stories and allegories about these beautiful birds, it's pretty simple for me. They give me hope, joy, and remind me of God's love. That's powerful enough to immediately impact my thoughts.

Now that he'd gotten my attention, I watched as the beautiful bird flew into the trees a few feet ahead of me. Awakened from my own dark thoughts for the first time, I noticed the trees were now brimming with cardinals, and the air was filled with their happy chatter. I'd never seen such a congregation of cardinals before and was completely awestruck.

I laughed and said a prayer of gratitude for the reminder of beauty, joy, and the gift of an uplifted heart. I immediately readjusted my thinking and saw everything through a different filter. The Enemies List evaporated and was replaced with thoughts of love and appreciation toward others.

It was quite a shift in my thinking!

That little cardinal now ranked toward the top of a new list. This one was a list of my "gratitudes" and included so many, many other blessings.

On another occasion, I needed to purchase some clothing items for a work event. It was a Saturday, and no one was available to help care for my husband at home. I dreaded our trip to the mall but felt I had no choice but to take EJ shopping with me.

At any time, managing public outings with EJ could be a bit difficult. I needed to pack up his walker, plan our route, navigate our way through the crowds, etc. Additionally, although he was generally in good spirits, his mood and behavior were unpredictable. Physically, things could change very quickly. He could lose stamina, freeze up and need to rest or use the restroom at unpredictable, inconvenient moments. The wheelchair was too heavy for me to manage in and out of the car, and I couldn't count on a courtesy one being available at the store. This meant he'd have to manage with his walker, which usually was an extremely slow and tiring experience for him.

As I prepared for the trip, I knew this day would be especially uncomfortable given Florida's high temperatures and humidity, both of which were already in the high nineties.

I grumbled the whole way to the mall.

Sadly, things did not improve once we arrived at our destination. All the handicap parking spots were filled and forced me to park some distance from the entrance to the store. We were both miserable as we slowly crossed the steamy lot. My husband complained of the heat and wanted to go home, well before we reached the entrance to the mall. I didn't blame him; I felt the same way, but decided to persevere, as we'd gone through so much effort already.

Once inside the well air-conditioned store, things became much more comfortable. Unfortunately however, there were no courtesy wheelchairs available. We would have to continue to rely upon him using his walker.

Although the store was quite busy, I had no concerns as we waited for the next elevator. We were surrounded by others, but the crowd didn't bother me at all. However, I hadn't anticipated that, as soon as the doors opened, my husband would unexpectedly and forcibly push his walker ahead of me. Walking with a burst of newfound speed I hadn't seen in a long while, he entered the elevator without me.

Regrettably, so did the rest of the crowd. The elevator quickly filled to capacity before I could enter and join my husband.

I called out, but it was too late. EJ had his back to the doors and I could see he was already engaged in a conversation with a stranger. He was blissfully unaware of the potential danger in the situation and seemed quite content as he chatted away with his new acquaintance.

My experience was considerably different from his; I was frantic as the doors closed. We were separated, me standing alone on the outside, EJ inside of the crowded elevator.

Frozen in place, I didn't know how to begin to get help. In the days before cell phones, some decisions weren't so easy. There was no way to contact him or immediately call for help. I was afraid to leave the spot in case he somehow returned to the last place we'd been together. I had no idea on what floor he might exit the elevator.

Will someone rush past him and cause him to fall? Will he wander away and get lost? How will I find him? How frightened he must be! All these thoughts raced through my mind while I prayed for guidance.

I was a wreck and couldn't think straight for some time, that is until I heard the next "ding" of the elevator.

After what seemed to be an eternity to me, but in reality, was probably only a few minutes, the elevator doors opened to reveal EJ and a stranger, a very pleasant man with incredibly kind eyes, talking together as if they'd known each other forever. I couldn't hear the content of their conversation, but my husband repeatedly referred to the gentleman as Buddy. They continued their jovial chat, as they slowly walked toward me. Anyone observing them would believe they were brothers or old friends, sharing a favorite story. I could see that EJ was completely at ease and enjoying his time with his newfound friend, unaware that the gentleman was in fact, a rescuer.

Perhaps "shepherd," in the sweetest sense, is a better description of EJ's new acquaintance.

Without taking the time to introduce himself, the gentleman explained that he had witnessed our separation as we tried to board the elevator. He apologized for it taking so long before they were able to return to me.

I quickly shifted from being stressed and confused to expressing my deep appreciation for his help. Most graciously, he rejected any notion that he deserved my thanks. And just as quickly as he'd stepped into our lives, the stranger slipped into the next vacant elevator and was gone.

"Well! It was sure good to see my buddy again," EJ said with a grin. "And I've had a good day, but I'm tired; let's go home."

And so, we did.

I learned a few lessons that day. There are truly angels around us; I already had everything I needed; and, when entering an elevator, always walk side by side with my husband so I don't fall behind in a crowd.

For these and so many other encounters with angels, I am truly thankful.

Simply by their loving acts, caregivers often provide inspiration and encouragement for others and are viewed as angels themselves.

If you're a caregiver, it may catch you by surprise when others share their feelings of respect and appreciation for you. Oddly, when I received these types of remarks, they often made me feel like a fraud. I seldom felt that I had done enough or made the right choices. I wondered, how could I possibly deserve such kind comments? Rather than protest or try to diminish their perceptions, I eventually learned to simply accept the sincerity of their comments.

Although I wasn't always aware of it at the time, my family and I continued to receive a multitude of blessings throughout the years following EJ's first admission to the hospital.

These blessings included encounters with loving individuals, job opportunities that met our family's ever-changing needs, as well as spiritual and medical professional support for my husband's recovery. I even encountered quite a few angels working at Veterans Affairs (but more about that another time).

From time to time, others have shared their stories of angel encounters with me. Each retelling of these events provided me with fresh inspiration and a deepened appreciation for the love that surrounds us all.

These messages of love and comfort continually renew my spirit:

How deep are the riches of the wisdom and knowledge of God! Romans 11:33

God's word is true from the beginning: and every one of his righteous judgements endures forever. Psalm 119

Lord, you have heard the desire of the humble: you will prepare their hearts, you will hear them. Psalm 10:17

For I know the thoughts that I think toward you, said the Lord, they are thoughts of peace, and not of evil, to give you an expected end. Jeremiah 29:11

Happy are those who trust in the Lord. Proverbs 16:20

In quietness, I find my strength and confidence. Isaiah 30:15

When I take the high ground, I maintain my strength and honor. In time, I will rejoice again. Proverbs 31:25

Set my affection on things above, not on things on the earth. Colossians 3:2

Blessed is the man that trusts in the Lord, and whose hope is in the Lord. Jeremiah 17: 7

Let us come before His presence with thanksgiving and make a joyful noise unto him with songs of gratitude and praise. Psalm 95:2

When love beckons to you, follow him, though his ways be hard and steep. - Kahlil Gibran

He heals the brokenhearted, comforts them, and binds up their wounds. Psalms 147:3

He shall cover you with his feathers, and you can trust that you are safe under his wings: his truth protects you, always. Psalms 91:4

He shall give his angels charge over me, to always keep me safe. Luke 4:10

Beloved daughter, rest safely in my arms; rest in my love; rest. These words often came into my thoughts as I struggled to overcome my worries. This message always brought me peace; it still does.

STEPPINGSTONES

∾ Things always take a turn for the better when I look up, instead of down; forward, instead of backward; and listen, instead of speaking.

∾ Love and joy are never far away, when I just change the direction that I'm looking toward.

∾ Accept the help and encouragement of others; it's Heaven-sent. By doing this, I am welcoming angels into my life.

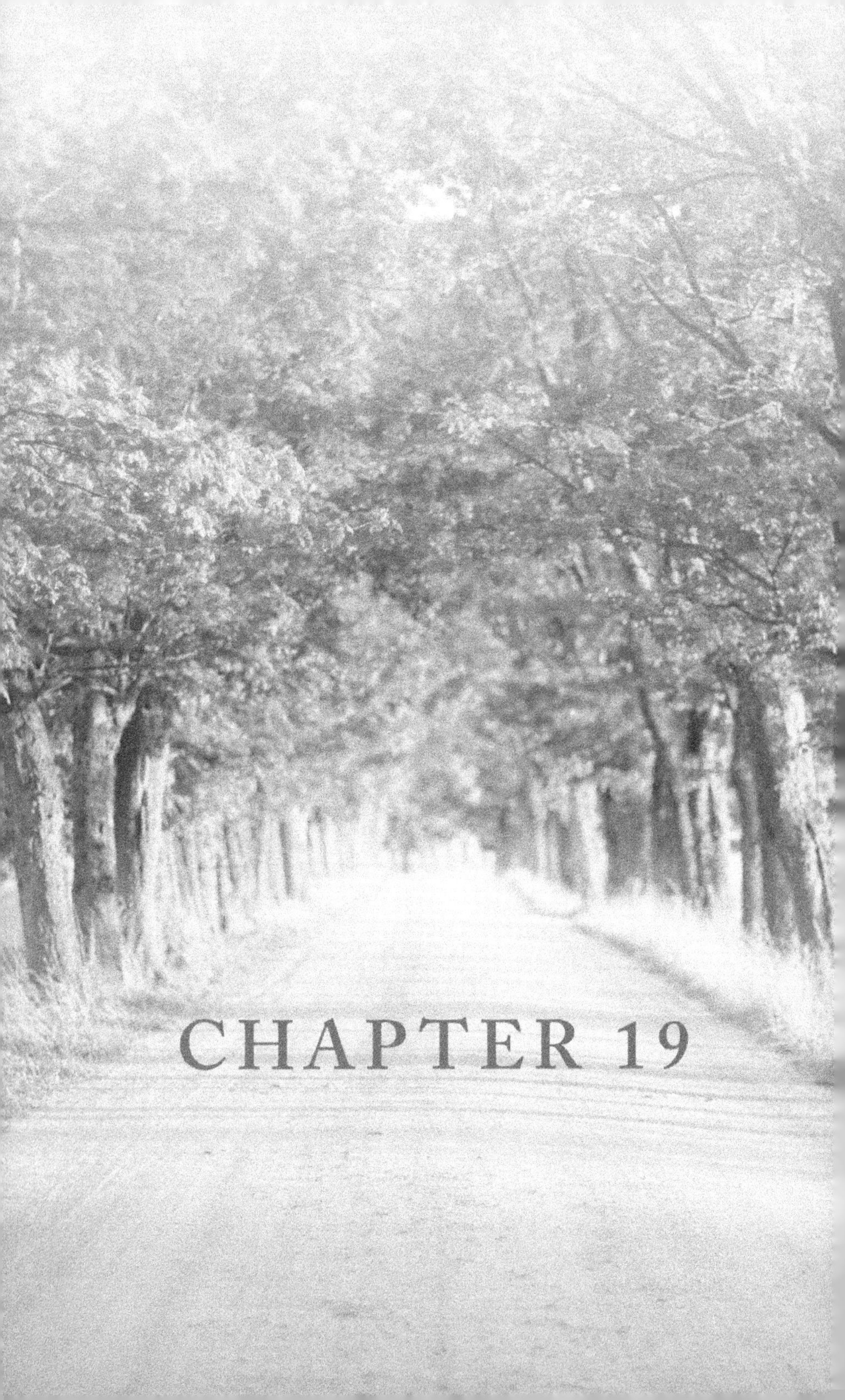

CHAPTER 19

Secrets, Fears and Tears

There is no place for fear in love; yet perfect love
casts out fear: because fear includes torment.
He that is afraid is not made perfect in love.
1 John 4:18

God is in charge. And God shall wipe away all
tears from their eyes; and there shall be no more
death, neither sorrow, nor crying,
neither shall there be any more pain:
for the former things are passed away.
Revelation 21:4

Courage is resistance to fear, mastery of fear,
not absence of fear.
- Mark Twain

"Do you ever pray that God will just take them away and that this will all be over soon?" the stranger next to me asked in a hushed tone, as she stared afar off.

It was sometime between two-thirty and four in the morning, that dark time when everything seems to rapidly shift between both the confusing and the chillingly clear aspects of life.

I'd been waiting hours for an update on my husband's condition from the emergency room doctors. I was not yet fifty years old, but already had several years of experience of dealing with these urgent medical events. I knew the drill by this time: the initial intake process, his thrashing, yelling, and striking out at the doctors until they sedated him, the tests, the waiting . . .

Even in the dismal, yellow grayness of the emergency room, I could also recognize another exhausted caregiver when we encountered each other.

Somehow, although we were strangers, there was no pretense between my fellow caregivers and me. We always spoke the naked truth with one another. Yet, we avoided eye contact while sharing some of our deepest, most intimate secrets. Baring our souls to strangers came easier than revealing these thoughts to our families and closest friends. Outsiders who were also caregivers had few judgments, and there was no fear of breaking a relationship, or experiencing any other repercussions, other than our own guilt, as a consequence for speaking our truth. However momentary these unfiltered thoughts and feelings might have been, sharing them offered some small bit of release from the pain.

Maybe that's how confessionals work best, with anonymous people who share a common experience, speaking their truth, and then you both move on. Knowing that you'll never have to acknowledge these deeply revealing conversations is a kindness in itself, I suppose.

"Yes, I've prayed for that, and I've done it more than once. But it's usually followed by my next prayer that He takes me instead. And then I feel deep regret and pray for forgiveness for both thoughts. Generally, I end up confessing that I'm just too weak to carry on, I'm bone tired and can't do this anymore. But somehow, I do; and I bet, somehow, you do too. And then my next prayer is one of gratitude, for one more day together. But yeah, I could skip times like these. I don't get it, why do any of us have to go through this? I think I'm losing my mind."

"Amen to that," the stranger beside me whispered.

We each sighed deeply as we retreated into our separate silent, private worlds and waited . . .

* * *

I often struggled with unfamiliar, ugly emotions.

As I listened to my few friends who were also caregivers, I discovered I wasn't alone in this. I knew these ladies to be sweet, loving, kind and generous. But at different points and caused by different events, all of us had been ambushed by difficult emotions we hadn't experienced before.

"I don't think I'd ever do it, but sometimes I really want to punch someone in the face when they go on and on about their perfect life, amazing husbands, or their fabulous vacations. I can't ever have those things again. Now that I think about it, maybe I will take out the next person who talks like that to me," said my always gentle, devout, and impeccably mannered friend.

She, too, was a long-term caregiver. No matter what she said, I knew her true nature and this wasn't it.

Still, I couldn't help but laugh out loud at the image of my friend, the consummate lady, Church-Going-Southern-Belle, with the ever-present pearl necklace, taking on some poor unsuspecting chatterbox. Although my friend laughed too, we both knew her feelings to be very real, at least on the bad days.

And we all had bad days.

I came to understand that irrational thoughts can still seem to have very real and harmful power if you let them. Sometimes, dark thoughts crept in when I saw couples doing things together. I'm not sure whether I was jealous or resentful of them, or maybe it was both. The day trips, the shopping, the date nights, sharing life with a fully engaged partner—I'd taken these simple things for granted.

Now, while I had so many things to be grateful for, I missed having a "normal" life with my other half. It was hard not to be envious of others who hadn't experienced a similar loss.

I learned not to suppress those harmful thoughts about others, but to recognize them for what they were. They were fiction; in my heart, I didn't really resent the happiness of others. Yet, recognizing the truth about myself and others was not always effortless. At times, I needed to remind myself that it wasn't my nature to be a hateful, jealous, or resentful person.

Never has been, never will be.

My pain had nothing to do with others, so how could I blame them? It wasn't always easy, but instead of focusing on my grievances, I shifted my thoughts to my list of "gratitudes". Nothing was too small to be included on this list.

Oftentimes, I felt that life with my husband was like trying to predict the movements of a hologram. What could be seen may not be real and shifted without notice.

It was very difficult and frequently impossible to predict his needs, emotions, and actions. His anger and the many ways it would be manifested were among the most difficult to foresee and manage.

I learned, if at all avoidable, not to argue with EJ although he may be telling a fantastic, untrue story or making a bizarre request. This wouldn't happen if he was in his right mind, so I didn't attempt to correct or argue with him when he was in the wrong mind.

You will never win these types of discussions. Their viewpoint is real to them, and you will not be able to convince them otherwise. The only thing you will accomplish is to agitate or further confuse your loved one.

Of course, there are times when taking a strong opposing stand is required. As difficult as it may have been, I tried to do so with patience and love.

For example, ignoring his left-side paralysis, EJ routinely insisted he knew the best therapy to enable him to run again. Several times a week, he tried to persuade one of us to securely loop a rope around his waist, tie it to the back bumper of the car and drive slowly until he was forced to run. He was obsessed with the idea and confident it would work.

No amount of reasoning could convince EJ this was a bad idea. He often became frustrated and angry when his request was denied. Eventually, I found a way to avoid upsetting him, yet standing firm that I would not be tying him to the car.

"Sorry, I can't do that because I'll go to jail," accompanied by a laugh, was the only response that worked with him. It usually elicited a chuckle in return. However, it was only a temporary solution. Several times a week he'd negotiate with different people to be a partner in his scheme; each time, of course, his request was denied. His obsessive attempt to gain a partner in this perceived best mode of therapy lasted for years. Engaging him in a different dialogue rather than treating him like a child was the best way to deflect his thoughts.

The next example of dealing with someone who perhaps is losing their grasp on reality is very tough to share with you. It still feels like a betrayal of trust between my husband and myself. Yet, sharing this extremely personal story may help another caregiver in some very important way.

That matters a lot to me.

Thankfully, doctors and therapists tried to prepare me in advance for the possibility of physical or verbal threats. They explained that these irrational events seem to flash out of nowhere. Still, it's frightening and emotionally draining when you're suddenly confronted with a potentially violent situation. One moment you're having a normal conversation, the next moment, your loved one is enraged and threatening to hit or otherwise harm you.

It's devastating; it's surreal, it's scary; and no one deserves this treatment— least of all, the one who is caring for the person.

I did experience these threats of violence. On a few occasions, my husband followed through on his threats. I'm so sorry if you experience this, too. Please do not keep this behavior a secret, as I did for some time.

There's no foolproof formula to handle these situations. But remember, you must always look after your own safety before taking steps to diffuse the situation.

All but a few times, I managed to totally reverse the seemingly inevitable course of events. I stayed calm and said, "I love you," and then I smiled. This was the magic elixir that usually calmed my husband and evoked a smile in return. I later learned that this strategy is called distraction. You may choose another way to distract the person you're caring for but try to stay calm while you're doing it.

The majority of times, the crisis passed without physical harm to me, but sometimes it didn't.

You may be reluctant to tell others of these incidents, whether they're just threats or actual physical abuse.

I was.

A lot of things worried me. I hoped the explosion was a one-off, an aberration, not worth mentioning. It was just one more thing to survive.

I often felt guilty that I may have done something to upset him. I also felt great compassion for my husband and didn't want others to know of this new behavior. Somehow, I wanted to protect him and myself from further scrutiny of our lives.

Additionally, I worried if others knew about his volatility and interactions with me, I'd be forced to confront the realities of the risk I was experiencing. I was afraid he would have to go into long-term care, and he'd be lost to me forever. I thought by keeping these violent bouts a secret, we could buy more time together.

I was willing to make that trade.

There may not always be an opportunity to use the deflection method to reframe the state of mind of the one you are responsible for, as in the situation I unexpectedly encountered while driving seventy miles an hour on a busy interstate.

It was Thanksgiving morning, and we were traveling for a few hours to join relatives for dinner. Moondoggy was included in the invitation, and since he usually did well on trips and around the family, we brought him along with us. I was very familiar with the two-hour route and didn't think twice about taking the dog with us. It was better than leaving him alone as it was going to be a very long day. And frankly, there were few other options, as no one was available to tend to him on the holiday.

There was no reason not to expect a smooth trip; however, from the moment we entered the interstate, Moondoggy became uncharacteristically agitated and barked loudly, with only a few momentary pauses. EJ, also out of character at this stage in his life, became enraged and yelled repeatedly at the top of his voice for the dog to shut up! He threatened horrible consequences if the barking didn't stop. Moondoggy's response was to bark louder and more frequently. This battle of wills went on for what seemed like a very long time. Eventually, I too yelled at them both to please stop.

Neither of them paid any attention to me; in fact, the situation only escalated.

Instead of calming down, EJ threatened, at the top of his voice, to get out of the car and make sure the dog stopped barking. He yelled at me repeatedly, "Let me out of this damn car!"

With his one functioning hand, he alternatively pounded the door and searched for a way to open it.

The situation was out of control and terrifying. I don't know what would have happened if I hadn't engaged the childproof locks before starting our journey!

Fortunately, I was able to navigate through the heavy traffic and make it to the next rest area just in time. Both my husband and the dog calmed down the minute the car stopped. Conversely, I sat there, holding onto the steering wheel and crying.

"What's wrong, Honey?" EJ asked, having no memory of the event that had just passed.

"Oh, I just heard a sad song. I'm okay." I lied, again. There was no point in revisiting the event. Instead, we put the leash on Moondoggy and headed for the dog walk area.

We spent quite some time walking and talking about random things before I had the courage to restart our journey.

The remainder of the trip was more normal than the start had been. There was no more barking, yelling or threatening to jump out of the car. However, because of the delay, our usual two-hour journey had now taken three and a half hours.

Upon our arrival, EJ got a warm, loving welcome; this was in stark contrast to the reception I received from his relatives. The family was agitated with our timing and questioned why we were so late. I had no opportunity to fake-blame the traffic before my husband gave his version of that morning's events.

"Oh, you know how Dianne is; she's always late. It doesn't seem to matter what's going on or who is waiting on her; she can't get her act together," my husband responded with a laugh. No one protested his comments, not even me. Instead, I put up with their withering looks and left EJ's insulting, unfair statements remain unchallenged.

Although EJ hadn't explained the morning's events accurately, he wasn't a dishonest or mean man. He simply had no memory of the morning's awful trip. Perhaps wrongly, I decided once again, to keep the truth to myself. Let his family think what they may, it was better than alarming them about his mental state, I decided.

Several weeks later, my visiting sister found me crying alone in the kitchen, following one very physical episode. I could no longer hide what had happened and told her the truth.

Shortly before her arrival, EJ had become infuriated while looking for his favorite snack in the pantry. When I told him we were out of the product he was looking for, he turned his anger on me. Shaking with rage, he raised his fist and held it just inches from my nose. Somehow, I dodged the intended blow, when he suddenly tried to punch me in the face with the full force of his fury.

"You hit me, and I'll have to let them put you away. You will never come home again. Is that what you want?" I yelled, for the first time ever.

Instantly, he froze in place, his face ashen. Then, we both broke down and sobbed. He continued to weep and apologize as I held him tightly and helped him go to bed. Shaken, I returned to the kitchen for some solitude and a strong cup of tea while I tried to process the encounter.

My sister, having just arrived for a visit, was totally unaware of the incident and had come upon me as I was struggling with one of the most difficult decisions of my life. I couldn't conceal the truth about EJ's violent outbursts any longer, and I shared it all with her.

She was crestfallen to learn the reality of our situation and firmly told me that the doctor should be aware of these incidents. She convinced me there may be other options than removing my husband from our home. She suggested, perhaps, a medication may need to be adjusted or there was something else going on with EJ that required attention.

She was right; thank God for sisters!

Thankfully, I was able to secure an appointment within a few days of the incident. The doctor adjusted his medications, and EJ had drastically fewer outbursts.

* * *

My childhood home was a busy, happy place. I don't recall any arguments or raised voices between my parents. Few words were necessary for my parents to express their emotions, and these few expressions were quite muted in tone.

An example of this is the way my mother addressed the issue of my younger brother loudly slurping his chicken noodle soup at the dinner table.

She quietly put down her soup spoon, took a deep breath, stared straight ahead, and posed the question, "Are we no better than the beasts?"

This was Big Drama, a serious rebuke, in our family. No one seated around our large dining room table spoke, yet her message hit its intended target. The dinner continued without a single further slurp.

Other than laughter, I never witnessed anyone in the family display a great deal of emotion, and most certainly, I never witnessed unrestrained tears.

Yet one day, I experienced something new. I had just turned thirteen, was alone in my room and just realized Ringo would never know I loved him. I began to have a good cry into my pillow.

I cried for a long time, not caring who heard me or what others might think. I couldn't stop, and I didn't care.

Eventually, Mom came in to check on me. I was too embarrassed to explain to her the reason for my tears, and her initial attempts to comfort me fell flat. When she realized I was inconsolable, she did something completely unexpected.

The same woman who exercised extreme restraint and dignity, regardless of the circumstances, encouraged me to cry, cry hard and get it all out of my system.

"Tears are just the melting of an internal iceberg. Don't be afraid of them. Stay here, cry all that you need to and let me know if you need anything. Join us when you're ready," she said, before slipping out of the room and closing my bedroom door.

My mother had given me permission to cry.

Feeling encouraged, I followed her guidance, wept until there were no more tears to cry and eventually rejoined the world, completely recovered.

"And anyway, if Ringo doesn't love me," I reasoned, "there's always the chance that Paul will."

Many years passed before I realized, in fact, that none of us needs permission to cry. It is a natural, healthy, and restorative act.

The Magical Crying Towel

Years ago, long before there were open conversations about mental health and available resources, I couldn't stop crying for three days. The specific circumstances that caused my tears don't really matter now. What's more important is what happened during that time.

Throughout those three days, I lost the desire or energy to do anything but stay in bed and weep. I ignored all attempts to help me, even with the basics like bringing me food and water. The voices of my family seemed far, far away. Only occasionally was I able to muster enough strength to respond to their suggestions with a slow nod of my head.

I wanted to go to sleep for a long, long time. I didn't want to hurt myself; I just wanted the pain to stop. Pulling deeper and deeper inside myself, I continued to reject all efforts for help.

My family was naturally, deeply concerned but were unsure of what to do to help me.

Eventually, and out of pure practicality, I made a trip to the bathroom. There, I picked up a clean towel before returning to bed. As the crying began again, I used one end of the towel to wipe my tears away and the other end to blow my nose.

Over the next few days, my only job was not to get the ends mixed up.

Well, what the hell. I'm still here, I thought on the morning of the fourth day.

I wanted a cup of tea in my favorite cup, stirred with (to me) the perfect little spoon. I got out of bed and struggled to make my way to the kitchen. I found comfort in the perfection of that hot, sweet, amber liquid.

One sip at a time, I put the cause and the prior days of pain behind me. They never had power over me again.

However, throughout the years following EJ's stroke, I did have occasion to use a crying towel again. These instances were few and far between, but when needed, the Magical Crying Towel served me very well.

So, my friend, should you ever question your need to cry, just follow your heart; you don't need to give yourself permission. And, if it helps, don't forget to use the mysterious healing of the Magical Crying Towel.

If you do, remember your only job is to keep the ends of the towel straight.

STEPPINGSTONES

∾ I'm stronger than I know. There are also times when I am weak; these times will pass, and I will experience personal progress because of these trials.

∾ Truth obliterates a lie. Remember and trust the truth about the real me.

∾ Sometimes, tears have their own healing power.

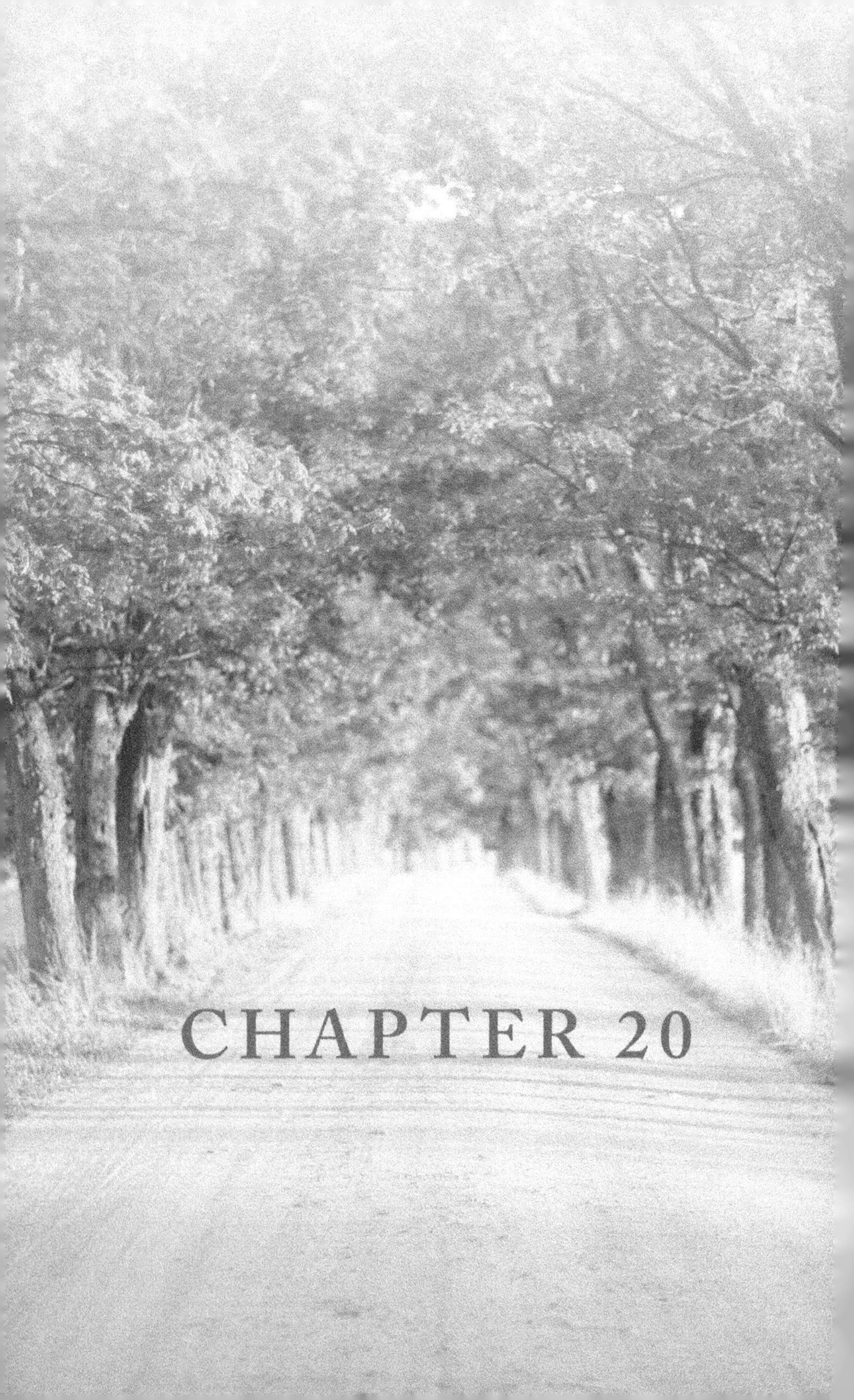

CHAPTER 20

The Second Call

Draw close unto God,
and he will draw close to you.
James 4:8

At all times and under all conditions, God is our
refuge and strength, a very present help in trouble.
Psalm 46:1

Divine Love always has met and
always will meet every human need.
- Mary Baker Eddy

Following yet another critical emergency medical event, EJ was admitted back into the hospital. He was now in his early sixties; I was in my late fifties. Weeks later and once his condition was stabilized, he was transferred to a skilled nursing facility. Thankfully, it was the most professionally run, cheerful, and clean facility I'd encountered during my husband's many years of care.

Throughout the two and half months of his stay, EJ seemed as content as possible with his surroundings and the staff. He was always in good spirits and appeared to be healthy during my visits. I believed he was making good progress, and we would soon be able to resume his care at home.

During our monthly meeting, I expressed my appreciation to the care team for all their concern and successful efforts to stabilize my husband's health. Unexpectedly, my comments were met with an awkward, momentary silence. I noticed that several of the team members seated around the table quickly shifted their gaze away from me.

The chairwoman of the meeting soon broke the silence and took the lead in the conversation. She explained that EJ's condition was not what it appeared to be to me.

According to the medical team, contrary to my personal evaluations based solely upon our limited interactions, my husband's dementia and Parkinson's disease were progressing rapidly. They continued to provide me with some of the details of his condition, which prohibited his return home. While I thought he had improved, they explained the opposite was the case. He now needed specialized care specifically for the memory and dementia issues. Additionally, his mobility issues were rapidly increasing and the use of a mechanical lift to get out of the bed was now required.

I probed for more information, thinking they had the wrong patient's records. But the team patiently explained to me I hadn't noticed this decline because he rallied during our visits, and I never saw him outside of his bed.

It was devastating to learn EJ probably would not be coming home again, ever. This time, I had no other choice but to accept their recommendations. I knew I could not physically provide the level of care at home that was needed at this point.

I was also informed the current facility was not approved for the specific kind of ongoing care my husband now required, and I had to find a new "home" for him. Further, I was made aware that the VA had already been informed of the impending discharge of my husband.

It was alarming to learn I had just two weeks to find a new residential care provider that met both the needed criteria for his care and was a VA-approved facility.

After confirming with our VA patient representative that the move was indeed required based upon EJ's medical status, I began a frantic search for a care facility within a hundred miles of our home.

The challenge to find a new facility was even more difficult because of the VA benefit coverage restrictions. Additionally, the waiting lists for these facilities were over two years long. I learned this was also true in non-VA-connected establishments.

The patient advocate made calls on our behalf too. But again, each facility we contacted informed us that the waiting lists were over two years long. The time was rapidly approaching for EJ to leave the existing facility, yet I had not been able to locate a new one for him.

I was at my wit's end and consumed with fear of the future. I truly didn't know what else I could do to locate a good, safe place for my husband. My nights were wracked with worry; my days were fraught with feelings of helplessness. I was exhausted and wanted to give up.

At last, I received a return call from a facility that was only twenty miles from home. The message stated there was an unexpected opening, but there were also several others on the waiting list.

I was informed that I would need to move quickly if I wanted to secure the room for him. I immediately set an appointment to tour the facility that afternoon.

In the meantime, as both the facility and area were unfamiliar to me, I researched the organization. I was much relieved to see the facility had the highest ratings awarded by the state of Florida. With high hopes and anticipation of a positive outcome, I asked my best friend to go with me. She agreed.

It promised to be a beautiful day, indeed. Or so I thought.

My friend and I were happy and chatty as we pulled into the parking lot. Yet, that all changed very quickly.

We could tell something was amiss the moment we stepped out of the car. We learned later the place was a very old, converted jail. There were few windows, and these were blocked by window air condition units. Unusual for this lush area of Florida, the grass was sparse, and there was no landscaping on the grounds. In spite of the few cars in the lot, it looked like a desolate, abandoned building.

Our shared glance as we approached the entry revealed our mutual sense of dread.

Once inside, we were greeted by a very friendly giant of a man with the very unusual name of Spartacus who would then give us a tour of the building.

Everywhere, patients in wheelchairs were parked side by side in dark hallways, many slumped over and seemingly unaware of the moans and distress of those around them. Occasionally, a patient would call out to Spartacus, seeking his attention. However, he continued the tour without pausing to interact with them.

It was impossible to ignore how the low ceilings didn't help dissipate the combined foul smells of urine and body odors. Patient rooms were small, crowded, without a natural light source, and seemed to be bathed in a perpetual blueish-green twilight.

I felt helpless to ease the suffering of the patients we encountered. I desperately wanted to bring in light and fresh air, as a start. I tried to mask my feelings but couldn't wait to leave such a sad, sad place.

Before saying our goodbyes, I commented on the state's ratings and asked our guide to explain theirs to me. Spartacus spoke sincerely and said the ratings included a good many compliance issues, such as postings, reports, accuracy with medications and the ratio of deaths to patient number. In closing, he stated that he was very proud of their administrative staff. There was no mention of the patients' actual quality of daily life.

I guess the state of Florida doesn't measure that.

Before parting, I shook Spartacus's hand and thanked him for his time. Neither of us spoke about the possibility of my husband moving into the facility. There was no need for explanation.

My friend and I didn't speak until we returned to the car. Too shaken to drive, I sat speechless, my head and my heart in complete turmoil as we remained in the car for what seemed to be an eternity.

Eventually, she broke the silence. "You can't do this!" she commanded, visibly distressed.

"I know, I know, I know!" I responded, while covering my face with my hands. I was gutted and still in no condition to drive.

Thankfully, after a few minutes of us crying, my sweet, bossy, beloved friend took over. She didn't give me a vote as she drove us straight to another facility, she had seen on her way to work. Along the way, I explained I had already contacted them and received the usual "sorry, we have a two-year waiting list" response. I was sure it would be a complete waste of time to just casually pop in and ask for a tour.

In spite of my explanation, she wasn't deterred and continued driving to the location. Did I mention my friend is tenacious, protective, and loyal? Oh, and double bossy!

I love her.

The Willows Care Center was an oasis with lovely landscaping, a tidy parking lot and inviting walking paths. The sun broke through the afternoon rain clouds, just as we arrived. The Spanish/Mediterranean building, so typical of Florida architecture, seemed to glow as the sunbeams bounced off the wet, tiled roof, soft yellow walls, and pristine sidewalk below. The surrounding bountiful flowers shimmered, still moist from their recent shower.

This has to be a good omen, I thought, even though I was afraid to be optimistic after our earlier experience. Yet, I was equally afraid to give up hope.

It was very surprising to me that, even without an appointment and with a long waiting list of prospective patients, we were warmly welcomed and immediately given a tour of the facility.

The Willows had a lovely residential feel and was bright and sunny. Each of the staff members we encountered made eye contact with us and greeted us in a professional manner. We passed a rather loud and competitive bingo game being held in one large room. Across the hall, one of the residents played the piano for a small gathering. Some of them clapped to the cheery Cole Porter tune, while others joined the group sing-along.

The hallways were busy with patients rolling about in their wheelchairs; several others gathered in the exterior courtyard to visit with each other. No one was "parked" and left on their own in a hallway. The only odors I detected were emanating from the cafeteria. Happily, these were pleasant and enticing.

The contrast to other facilities I'd visited was dramatic. It was clean, cheerful, and appeared to be staffed with professionals. I was convinced that this was the perfect spot for EJ. Yet, unfortunately, I could do no more than add his name to the waitlist before we said our goodbyes to our guide.

My friend was right to insist that we stop at The Willows. Although I had no hope that EJ would be admitted there, I now had a benchmark to aim for while searching for a new "home" for my husband.

In the days that followed, I was under constant pressure to find another facility for my husband. I was running out of time and didn't know what was going to happen next. Even with the help of the social workers from both the VA and the current facility, nothing could be found that fit our needs. It was a very difficult time. I couldn't sleep, it was hard to work and I was wrung out with worry.

I had no solutions and no other ideas. I begged God for guidance.

Inwardly, I continually prayed to overcome my fears. Additionally, I prayed to be strong enough to keep my hope from waning, no matter the seemingly unending challenges, twists, and turns I encountered. There were many times I just wanted to give up but eventually found great comfort in knowing that God—not me—was in charge, as always.

The pattern of my life included going to work, going to see EJ, praying that everything would work out before his time was up at the current facility, trying to find a new place that would take him, begging for help, talking with the kids while pretending everything was fine, eating dinner around nine, trying to sleep, waking up late, rushing to work, attempting to segregate my personal problems from my professional responsibilities, continuing to be a resource for others while barely able to face each day myself . . .

Lather, rinse, repeat. Lather, rinse, repeat.

Exhausted from praying continually for an answer to our problems, I finally shifted my thoughts from begging for mercy and help, to truly realizing that the plan was already in place; it just hadn't been revealed to me yet.

This brought me great comfort.

Quite early one morning as I was preparing to go to work, I received a phone call from a stranger.

"Mrs. Allen, this is Mr. Jones with The Willows Care Center. Are you still interested in having your husband join us? We have an opening, but I have many others on the list. Are you able to give me your answer now?"

"Yes! Yes! Yes! God bless you. Yes! Mr. Jones, you're an angel! Are you sure this isn't a mistake? Do you have the right Mrs. Allen? It's a pretty common name; please double-check."

Mr. Jones confirmed EJ's personal data and assured me that the vacancy was ours if we wanted it.

"But how did that happen? I thought there was a two- year waiting list." I was still in a state of shock and was afraid to fully trust this exceptionally good news.

"I couldn't say, but does it really matter? I'm happy to save the room for your husband. I would advise that you arrange for him to transfer over this afternoon. And, Mrs. Allen, we look forward to having him with us." His voice was so calm and sweet; I believed in the sincerity of his welcome.

We then completed the necessary details for the immediate transfer of my husband to his new home-away-from-home.

After we hung up, I was overwhelmed with gratitude and fell to my knees, weeping with joy. I thanked God for his abundant care and blessings. Somehow, this morning's impactful events didn't interfere with my ability to get to work on time.

By late that afternoon, all the details were handled and the transfer to The Willows was complete. EJ was safely and happily snuggled down in his new surroundings.

He would soon come to regard his stay at the Willows as a vacation. It took me a while to understand that he believed he was staying in a hotel.

EJ explained to me that he liked to spend his free time in the "lobby" watching everyone come and go. He thought the nurses' station was the front desk. He'd tell me how surprised he was that more of his fellow guests didn't speak French but was very pleased to discover that the many beautiful Haitian women who worked there were happy to speak with him. Somehow, between French, Patois and English, they managed to communicate with each other perfectly.

Indeed, my prayers had been answered; my husband was safe, cared for and happy.

STEPPINGSTONES

∞ Our God who parted the Red Sea will most certainly lead us through this challenging time.

∞ We are cared for, provided for and safe in His arms.

∞ God's ways are beyond my understanding; how grateful I am for His loving care.

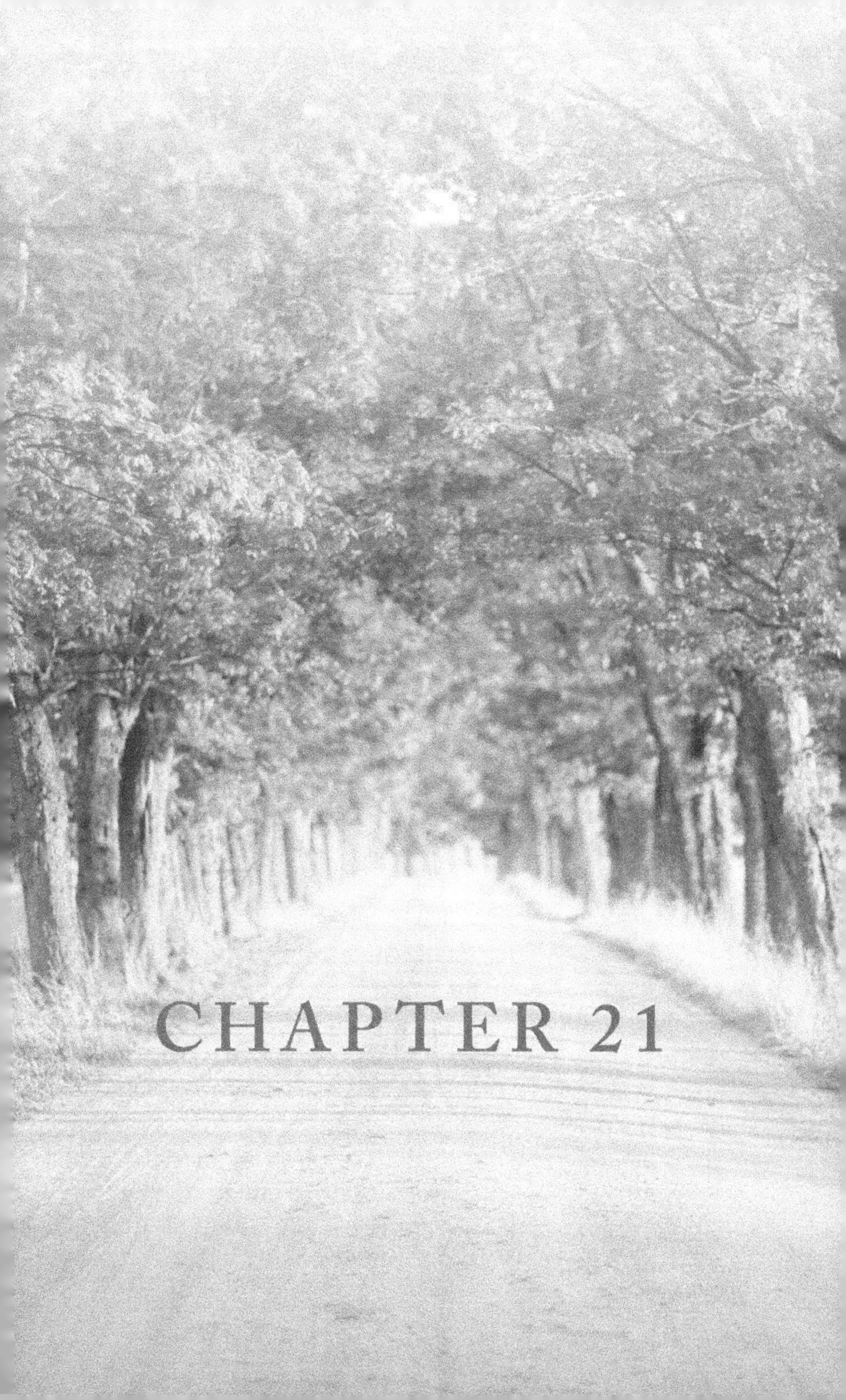

CHAPTER 21

The Third Call

*His lord said to him, you've done well, my good
and faithful servant; you have been faithful over
a few things, I will make you ruler over many
things: now enter into the joy of your lord.*
Matthew 25:23

A phone call before seven in the morning is never a good sign.

As tired as I was, the ringing of the phone cut through my grogginess and made me anxious. A man's calm, but firm voice on the other end of the call explained that my husband was found unresponsive during their morning rounds. He quickly continued, stating an ambulance was on its way and asked if I had a preference between the local hospitals. While trying to remain composed, I answered his questions and began the preparations for the trip to the hospital.

Unfortunately, I knew the process all too well. I started to go down the mental checklist of what needed to be done next and what would be required for his admission to the hospital. Placing the large tote bag at the end of the bed, I tried to kick it into gear and start packing, but I kept getting blocked from making progress.

No matter how positive an outlook I tried to maintain, I couldn't ignore my pounding heart nor my intrusive fears.

My husband's care at the Willows during the past year had been everything I'd hoped for him. Yet, although quite painful, I had to acknowledge that EJ's physical and mental decline had taken a dramatic downturn in the last few months. I feared this call meant something more serious than those of the past. I struggled to function and get ready to go to the hospital, but I just couldn't manage even the most basic tasks.

So, I did the most important thing. I sat down and prayed.

I prayed for EJ's safety, comfort, and protection. I prayed for those who would be treating him. I prayed for my children and myself, that we would once again be able to rise to the occasion and do what needed to be done, without completely broken hearts.

No matter how I tried to resist, my prayers were interrupted with racing, random thoughts of those nagging to-do- lists I'd come to rely upon so many times.

"Don't forget to check the Go-kit, call the kids and, this time, remember to ask Cindy to check on the pets."

I was drowning in mental chaos and then without explanation, things shifted. I suddenly experienced an enveloping calmness.

While sitting in silence and listening for guidance, I humbly recalled the prayer that is known to always work, and I willingly submitted to its power.

"Thy will be done . . ."

Though we were miles apart at that moment, I instantly felt an incredibly strong connection to my husband and spoke directly to him.

"My Love, you've fought the good fight. I'll be okay; the kids will be okay. You are a good man. You've done your job, and you are loved more than you will ever know. Sweetheart, mission accomplished. You've earned your rest."

I remained there in silence, alone with my thoughts. After a few moments, the phone rang again. This time, a woman's beautiful, soothing voice was on the other end of the call.

"Mrs. Allen, I'm so sorry, but the EMTs couldn't revive your husband. He has passed over. We'll keep him here until you arrive."

She continued, while I tried to focus on her words through my flood of emotions.

"I want you to know I've never seen someone so peaceful and beautiful at this time. Mrs. Allen, he passed with a smile on his lips."

And so he did.

* * *

My journey as a caregiver was now completed.

It started without warning and ended in its own time. Although I'd been imperfect at the job, I'd had many victories as well. It didn't matter whether I was willing or ready, the next phase of my life had already begun.

Ah, but that's a story for another time.

Dearest Reader, if you are a caregiver, hold one close in your heart or simply know of one, my hope is that their journey ends because the one they care for has experienced a complete recovery to a health-full life. If that is not the case, help them to know there is life and love yet to be experienced.

Mission accomplished and now it's time to take on another role.

Whatever path your journey takes, I pray that, along the way, much love and joy are part of the experience, as it was with mine.

Unable are the loved to die,
for love is immortality.
Emily Dickinson

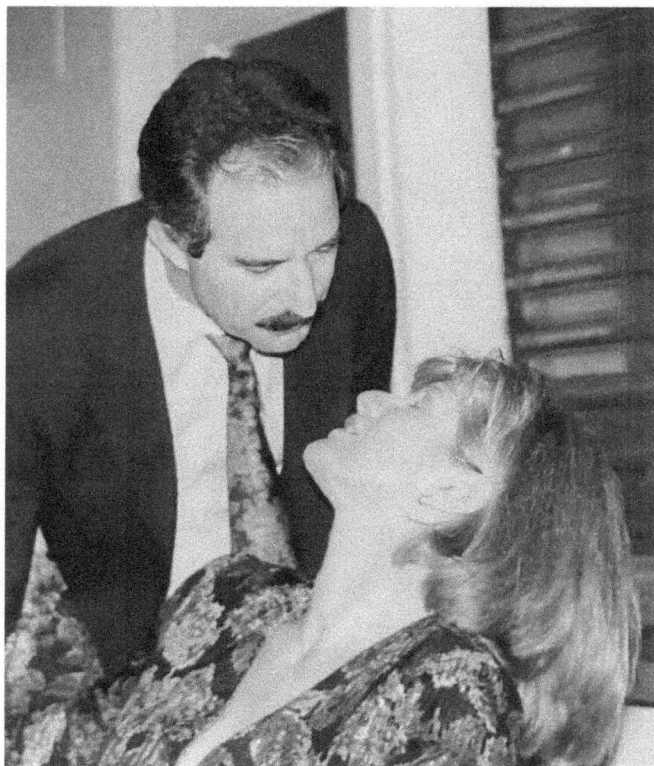

July 25, 1994

Milestones

- I don't get to choose what comes my way, but I can choose how to respond to each challenge.

- It's not rude to stand firm against aggressive, ill-intentioned people. It's not only my right, but also my duty to protect my loved ones from such as these.

- Pray without ceasing and trust that God will always give me the strength and guidance to do what I need to do; I am sustained by this faith.

- Be grateful for God's love and all that entails, in *advance* of my need. Begin each day with Psalm 118:24. "This is the day the Lord has made; let us rejoice and be glad in it." End each night with the Lord's Prayer, understanding that the first word is *Our* and include everyone in my prayers.

- I am now an activist for my husband's care and well-being! It's not important that I know it all; it's important that I give it my all. I'm not superhuman, and I'm better for knowing this. Sometimes, I need help and advice to figure this all out.

- Bring in the light and the joy, no matter the situation! And remember, don't sweat the small stuff.

- I'm in new and unfamiliar territory. Although it may be difficult, it's safe to let the professionals guide me through these challenging times.

- By definition, "trial and error" means I'm going to get it wrong sometimes. My job is to try to maintain the right balance between the two and learn from any mistakes.

- Stop being afraid and feeling overwhelmed; I can do this! Understand when we need help and adjust to these changing circumstances. When others want to help, don't be shy about letting them know *how* they can help.

- Set boundaries with others whenever necessary. Forgive them and move on.

- Everything is changing. It's often a bit scary, but there's also a new freedom that comes with accepting this truth. No matter the circumstances, stay true to myself, true to my values.

- What a blessing it is to have someone to dream with, to laugh with, to know so well and to care about, oh so very well. Our small, lovely world brings the most joy to me. The simple things bring so much joy to us both! I treasure the blessings of these times together.

- Things always take a turn for the better when I look up, instead of down; forward, instead of backward; and listen, instead of speaking. Love and joy are never far away when I just change the direction I'm looking toward.

- Accept the help and encouragement of others; it's Heaven-sent. By doing this, I am welcoming angels into my life.

- I'm stronger than I know. There are also times when I am weak; these times will pass, and I will experience personal progress as a result of these trials.

- Trial and error are not failures. They are building blocks to a better way, a better solution. Be kind to myself when they feel like stumbling blocks. "Suck it up, Buttercup," get back on my feet and try again.

- I need to pivot from "the way things used to be" to "the way things can be" and make the most of each new situation.

- Healing is often invisible; recovery isn't always linear. I can't be discouraged just because I don't see progress at the moment.

- Control my temper, even if my anger feels justified at the time. In the long-term, it's better for my well-being, and I don't have to live with the regret of my failing. I need to look for better ways to get the results I seek and have the presence of mind to do it in real-time.

- Listen, listen, listen! When making difficult decisions, gather as much information as possible, discuss the issues with those who can best guide me and include those who will be affected by my decision. Try to be objective and, ultimately, pray hard and just do the best I can.

  That's all anyone can ask.

- Be transparent with those I love and ask for the same in return. No matter how painful, we can bear the truth together.

- Know our rights to fair, honest, and respectful treatment and when necessary, hold my ground on these entitlements. Confront issues, not people. I have the strength through God to know what's true and to do what's right.

- It's not selfish to follow my own advice to others about self-care. It's the oxygen needed to keep me going. Start by shutting out feelings of inadequacy, fear, and anger.

- My soul, my spirit, my mind, and my heart need nourishment at all times. Some days more is required than on others. Yet, I'm not afraid of doing this work, for I am not alone. I can do this one step at a time. And by taking care of myself, I can better take care of others.

- Our God who parted the Red Sea will most certainly lead us through this challenging time. We are cared for, provided for and safe in His arms.

- God's ways are beyond my understanding; how grateful I am for His loving care.

- To love and to know that I am loved, is the greatest blessing of all.

Acknowledgments

For their endless love, patience, and helpful insights, I wish to thank my beloved immediate and extended family, my husband Robert Rodriguez, children John and Rachel Collins, Lynn and Jennifer Greene-Rooks, Tom and Michelle Rooks, brothers and sisters Susan and David Leitch, Bob and Nan Pittman, John and Anne Pittman, Max and Angie Pittman, Steve Pittman, Julie Wood, family by choice Daniella and Eddie Feuerstein, as well as Mike and Susan Iwuc.

Additionally, I appreciate the guidance and encouragement of Ellen Adelman, Dorothy Beek, Dawn Brotherton, Navolia Bryant, Margaret Callahan, Monica Frey, Cynthia Holland, Toby Johnson-Ramirez, Jan Ledbetter, Jane McFerrin, Jessica Quiles, Rosalyn Smith, Judith Welty, and Cy Young.

For their kindness and support throughout the most difficult times of my journey as a caregiver, I wish to express my gratitude to Jim Brown, Vi Dixon, Jan Keeler-Vincent, Richard Kessler, Hans Maissen, Atef Mankarios, Joy Rothschild, Robert Stanfield, Jeff Wagner, Philip Wood and so many other friends, neighbors, and colleagues.

My heart is filled with gratitude for each and every one of you.

Thank you; thoroughly, thoroughly thank you!

Topics and Questions for Discussion

1. What do you like the most and the least about An Imperfect Caregiver's Journey?

2. Are there any scenes that you particularly enjoyed or that made you uncomfortable?

3. "Life was perfect...who wouldn't want to be me; who wouldn't want to be us? And then without warning, everything changed." Over time, in what ways did the author's perception of a perfect life change? Is perfection an illusion? Were any of her versions of the "perfect life" achievable and sustainable?

4. What is your view of a "perfect life"?

5. Share a favorite scene or passage from this book. Why does it resonate with you?

6. Do you believe that the act of acknowledging her imperfections was a necessary part of the author's journey as a caregiver, as well as her personal growth? How so?

7. Have you been thrust into, or know of someone who has experienced, an unexpected life change? What were the challenges, the discoveries, and the resultant growth of these experiences?

8. Did this book cause you to reflect upon your own life or the experiences of others? How?

9. What impressions do you have of the author as a wife, as a mother, as a daughter, as a friend? Did your opinions change as your reading progressed?

10. Learning to be a caregiver isn't easy. What would you have done differently?

11. What questions would you like to ask the author? Are there any questions you would like to ask other characters?

12. Do you find the story relatable and authentic?

13. In addition to dealing with a cataclysmic health event and all that entails, the family was confronted with several other difficult trials. Considering their experiences separately, what were these issues?

14. What's your opinion of how the family met their challenges?

15. How did the journeys of the author and her husband differ? How were their experiences similar?

16. An Imperfect Caregiver's Journey is a highly personal account of challenges faced by the author regarding

faith, addictive behaviors, relationships, and physical issues; yet the author claims to be a very private person. What do you believe is her motivation in sharing this story? How well do you believe her goal was accomplished?

17. Have you learned anything new about the experiences of caregivers and those in their charge? What?

18. Many "tips and hacks" are offered throughout the book. Have you gained any new practical knowledge? If so, what, and how will you use the information?

19. Have you had experiences that required you to address difficult situations with people of authority or those with whom you have personal relationships? How did that go for you?

20. "What would a nice person do?" How do you show support for others in their time of need? How have others demonstrated their care for you?

21. Do you agree with the examples of "Alarm Bells"? Would you add anything else or subtract something from the list?

22. How do you feel about the author's choices to confront others when she viewed them as offensive, dismissive, or negatively impacting her husband's experience? Give an example and share how you felt about the situation.

23. On a variety of topics, the author elected to withhold some information from family, friends, and employ-

ers. What were they and do you agree with her decisions? Why or why not?

24. "Our personal communion with God is the most intimate relationship we will ever have." How did the author's spiritual journey evolve? What were some of the changes in her beliefs and what remained constant for her? If you care to share, have you had similar experiences?

25. Which passages impacted you emotionally? What are they and what feelings did they provoke?

26. Are there any scenes that you chose to reread or continued to reflect upon?

27. Following his initial critical health event, how did the relationships and roles between the husband and wife change? What, if anything, remained the same?

28. Do you like the author's style? Did the story engage your interest and move along easily? Or did you find the pace slow and uninteresting?

29. How has this book affected your perspective or how you go about your life? Did the story make you want to further explore this area of human experience?

30. Will you recommend this book to others? Who are they and why would you suggest they read An Imperfect Cargiver's Journey?

Share this Healing and Loving Mission

Thank you for reading, *An Imperfect Caregiver's Journey.*

I hope you will join me in providing comfort and inspiration for others. One way to help is through book reviews, as reviews are the metric used to further the message and connect with new readers.

Please consider taking a moment to leave a review to help others choose their next book.

ASIN: B0CZJP48TW

About the Author

Photo credit: Corey Miller

Wife, mother and long-term caregiver, Dianne Allen is a self-described and proud "Navy Brat" who grew up in San Diego, California. She now resides in New Braunfels, Texas with her beloved husband Robert Rodriguez and their ever-playful dogs Lily and Daisy. She is a former Vice President of Human Resources (HR) for international luxury hotel companies, a former adjunct professor, and a current HR consultant. An avid writer, Dianne has written multiple articles regarding spirituality and faith. She has also created programs and films focused on leadership development and organizational cultural which have been utilized throughout the hospitality industry. An Imperfect Caregiver's Journey is her first memoir.

www.diannegallen.com
Dianne.allen.author@gmail.com
Instagram: diannegallen